D0502690

Mayhem

Mayhem

SIGRID RAUSING

Alfred A. Knopf
NEW YORK   2017

THIS IS A BORZOI BOOK
PUBLISHED BY ALFRED A. KNOPF

Copyright © 2017 by Sigrid Rausing

All rights reserved. Published in the United States by Alfred A. Knopf, a division of Penguin Random House LLC, New York, and distributed in Canada by Random House of Canada, a division of Penguin Random House Canada Limited, Toronto. Simultaneously published in hardcover in Great Britain by Hamish Hamilton, an imprint of Penguin Random House Ltd., London.

www.aaknopf.com

Knopf, Borzoi Books, and the colophon are registered trademarks of Penguin Random House LLC.

Grateful acknowledgment is made to the following for permission to reprint previously published material:

Alfred Publishing, LLC: Lyric excerpt from "The Carnival Is Over," words and music by Tom Springfield, copyright © 1965 by Chappell Music Ltd., copyright renewed. All rights reserved. Reprinted by permission of Alfred Publishing, LLC.

Hal Leonard LLC: Lyric excerpt of "The Big Rock Candy Mountain," words and music by Burl Ives, copyright © 1949 by Universal Music Corp., copyright renewed. All rights reserved.

Lyric excerpt of "Jacob and Sons," from *Joseph and the Amazing Technicolor Dreamcoat*, music by Andrew Lloyd Webber, lyrics by Tim Rice, copyright © 1969 by The Really Useful Group Ltd., copyright renewed. International copyright secured. All rights reserved. Reprinted by permission of Hal Leonard LLC.

Library of Congress Cataloging-in-Publication Data
Names: Rausing, Sigrid.
Title: Mayhem / Sigrid Rausing.
Description: First edition. | New York : Alfred A. Knopf, 2017.
Identifiers: LCCN 2016052496 (print) | LCCN 2016053877 (ebook) |
ISBN 9780451493125 (hardcover : alk. paper) | ISBN 9780451493132 (ebook)
Subjects: LCSH: Rausing, Sigrid—Health. | Drug addicts—Biography. |
Drug abuse—Biography. | Families—Biography.
Classification: LCC RC566.R39 2017 (print) | LCC RC566 (ebook) |
DDC 362.29092 [B] —dc23
LC record available at https://lccn.loc.gov/2016052496

Jacket photography by Daniel Hotz
Jacket design by Carol Devine Carson

Manufactured in the United States of America
First Edition

For L, S, J, and T

Perhaps one did not want to be loved so much
as to be understood.

—George Orwell, *Nineteen Eighty-Four*

Mayhem

I

Now that it's all over I find myself thinking about family history and family memories; the stories that hold a family together, and the acts that can split it apart.

I used to think that no act was irreversible; that decisions taken and mistakes made could, on the whole, be put right. Now I know that certain acts in life are irreversible and lead you to landscapes you never dreamt of.

*

There is a repeated line in August Strindberg's play of 1902, *A Dream Play:* "Det är synd om människorna." The line is spoken by the god Indra's daughter, who descends to earth in order to better understand humanity and its self-inflicted suffering. The expression is not easy to translate. Edwin Björkman, in his early-twentieth-century translation of the play, rendered it plainly, but perhaps slightly awkwardly, as "Men are to be pitied." *Det är synd om människorna.* And of all the self-inflicted wounds of humanity, addiction, it seems to me, is one of the most tragic. Who can help the addict, consumed by a shaming hunger, a need beyond control? There is no medicine: the drugs *are* the medicine.

And who can help their families, so implicated in the self-destruction of the addict? Who can help when the very notion of "help" becomes synonymous with an exercise of power; a familial police state; an end to freedom, in the addict's mind?

This is a story about witnessing addiction. In some ways it's an ordinary story: two people, Hans and Eva, my brother and his wife, met in recovery, fell in love, got married, had children, then relapsed. He survived; she did not. Addiction stories are the same the world over—the individuality of addicts is curiously erased by the predictable progress of the disease and of recovery.

In our case, what made the story different was partly the fact that it became so public. Witnessing the apparently voluntary physical and mental decline of people you love is inexpressibly painful. In that context, whether the story is public or not doesn't matter: the sadness and anxiety are so overwhelming that headlines are irrelevant. But you don't want the media to own the story of your life.

That might be a good enough reason to write a book. But I had also always assumed that when dramatic events occur, there would be a narrative, followed by a conclusion, to be filed in the family archive. The story would be told, probably by lawyers; facts would be revealed, and future generations of the family would know what happened.

But it turned out that no one was collating the facts. There was no timeline and no coherent family narrative. And yet Hans and Eva's addiction was the worst thing that had ever happened to us. It dragged us to the underworld of mute slow-motion grief, the realm of sudden breakdowns and uncanny delusions. It brought us rounds of disturbing disputes; time-consuming and complex exchanges of emails; endless reports and conversations; engagements with psychiatrists, therapists, and addiction experts of every kind. It made me think deeply about the nature of family and the limits of our responsibility for one another; who we were, and who we had become.

Hans and Eva got married in 1992. It was the culmination of years of recovery. They had gone to 12-step meetings; they had sponsors, they may even have sponsored others, and they gave money to addiction charities. By 1999, they had three children. Then, eight years after they got married, they had a catastrophic relapse.

It lasted for twelve years. I was thirty-eight when it began; fifty when it ended.

I want to understand how it all began, long before the relapse. But who knows how, or why; what prehistory of emotions, or predestination of genes, leads people into addiction.

I know some things. In the early 1980s, Hans, aged eighteen or nineteen, travelled with friends by train through the Soviet Union, China, and India. In Goa they met some young Italian women staying on the beach: that was his introduction to heroin.

Eva was an expat American, born in Hong Kong, raised in England. She became a drug addict when she was even younger than Hans.

There were many rehabs along the way. In the late 1980s they happened to go to the same place. At this point they hadn't met. Eva was further on in her recovery and had already left

when she was asked by the rehab to persuade Hans to stay on—
he was close to walking out, back into drugs. She had a knack,
it seemed, of helping fellow addicts, and she did talk him into
staying. They became friends.

Some time later—they were more than friends now—Hans
took Eva down to my parents' house in the country to meet
the family. I remember her well, at that first meeting. She was
leaning against the back of the library sofa in a pink Chanel
suit; blond, thin, and a little guarded. She looked simultaneously
young and old, conventional and wild, groomed and unkempt.
She had grown up in London, but she seemed more American
than English to me. Her mother was from North Carolina; her
father had come to America from Europe quite young.

My mother knew them; they had attended the same Families Anonymous group in Chelsea.

*

I heard the writer David Grossman once, talking about griev-
ing for his son who had died, tragically, in one of Israel's many
conflicts. He said that putting words to emotions is what makes
us human. I wanted to add, or perhaps he said, that if you fail
to *make sense* of grief, it can turn you into something other than
what you are, or what you were. Writing is a form of making
sense.

I believe in writing. I am an editor and a publisher; text is
my profession. Reading, and writing, can make us consider our
emotions, who we love, and why, and how. I know I love my
brother, not because he deserves it (who does?), but because
since we were teenagers when I catch his eye I want to laugh;

because his being is so authentic and his presence (his height, his bulk, his spirit) so comforting again after the long hiatus, the spell in the wilderness, the zombie status.

My brother told me a year or so ago that he was reading Proust's *In Search of Lost Time.* For the second time I omitted to tell him about this book, my own memory project. The first time was some months earlier, when he asked me if I was writing. My last book, a memoir about living for a year on a Soviet collective farm, had just been short-listed for a small prize, and he was pleased, I think, and happy for me. It was my mother's birthday; I stalled for time, vague, evasive. At some point during the dinner I started singing. Dinners with my parents mean songs; it is the Swedish way. The children catch one another's eyes and laugh, as they do and have done, year in, year out.

Thus my brother and I used to catch each other's eyes when we were small and again when we were teenagers.

My mother smiles and hums, tunelessly. My father hums, and sings, tunelessly. My brother joins in too. Then suddenly he smiles an unexpectedly sweet smile and waves a little to my friend Johanna's young daughter, who is lying on a sofa watching a DVD, watching us, and suddenly I am crying, thinking of all the time Hans lost with his own children, and singing too, tasting the salty tears in my mouth.

I know that salty flavour well.

It was poignant, that long blue May evening, those Swedish songs in the Sussex countryside. We sang on until my father choked and had to leave the table, leaning heavily on me as we slowly walked back to the library, and his chair.

My brother looked away, pained.

. . .

In Search of Lost Time. I will try not to be melodramatic. But this story is so inherently dramatic that to tell it at all threatens to become an act of vulgarity; a descent to sententious and sensational tabloid mores. There has been enough of that—there was even a Swedish opera, staged in 2016, trying, and failing, to catch the meaning of what happened. *Death* is a character in the libretto, doubling as a drug dealer. The text insinuates that my brother's addiction was a form of revenge against my grandfather's insatiable greed; his desire for wealth and dynasty.

"To be a visionary was never good enough for him. You should have wealth, and a dynasty too," the character who is supposed to be Eva sings.

Hans responds: "And my revenge was living the life of a drug addict. A source of shame for my entire family."

Eva: "You resisted! You refused!"

My sister Lisbet and I are portrayed as the dark Norns of Holland Park—those female beings of Norse mythology who spin the fates of ordinary mortals. We turn our dark heads like vultures; we take Eva's children.

If you do not tell your stories others will tell them for you, and they will vulgarize and degrade you, said Ishmael Reed, quoting George Bernard Shaw.

I write, knowing that writing at all may be seen as a betrayal of family; a shaming, exploitative, act. Anyone reading this who thinks so, please know that I thought it before you. Anyone reading this who thinks so, consider also how we were brought up: wealth, privacy, silence, discretion.

But someone died, early one morning or late one night.

Eva was, I think, on her way to recovery when she died. There were signs that she was coming back. And yet she died.

Too many addicts are dying; too many families are broken.

*

"Mayhem" is an old English legal term for the crime of maiming. The term implies guilt, which is appropriate in this context, since there is no addict story that doesn't revolve around guilt, shame, and judgement. The guilt is indiscriminate, and so is the shame. We were all guilty, and we were none of us guilty. We were all shamed, and we absorbed that shame.

We played our parts. "Addict," "family members." Like all families torn apart by addiction, we came to know the steps of that intricate dance.

2

For some time now I have been seeing a psychoanalyst. I wrestle with my memory in the sessions; my dreams dissipate unless I write them down the minute I wake up, reaching for my glasses, eyes not quite open. Sometimes I write with my eyes closed. Then I forget what I have written and stare at my half-illegible handwriting, trying to reconstruct what is lost.

Memories are the essence of psychoanalysis, and I am aware, having done this before, of how little I now remember. In each session I try to remember what we talked about the day before, or the week before. I want to restore continuity to what otherwise threatens to become a jagged sequence of images and sounds with no order, no meaning, and no sense.

Thinking about this I realise that much of my adult life has been devoted to memory. I plant memories in houses, letters in random drawers, notes that I might come upon in old age, messages from now to then, the land of the unknowable.

My other books, too, were at least partly about memory. The first was academic, based on anthropological field research in a remote village in post-Soviet Estonia; the second was a memoir based on the year I lived there. The relationship between political repression and individual memory was central to both of them. How much do people remember if history is censored? Not that much, it turned out. Memories of Stalinism, and of Estonian independence before that, were fragmented in the village, the centre of a former collective farm—whole worlds were lost. It fascinated me, that loss, perhaps because I partially lost a world too, when I moved from Sweden to England in 1980. A world still remembered by my mother, who knew every well-known name in Sweden, every family connection, every family tragedy and success.

Who will remember Sweden for me when she is no longer here?

Memory is a family preoccupation. My father's brother Sven, who may have been autistic, had savant memory capacities. He spoke thirteen languages and could mimic many more; he was said to know the name of every church in Sweden and the precise distance between all major European towns. He laughed a somewhat frightening hysterical laugh and was emphatic, at times phobic, about his likes and dislikes.

I remember his great annual January birthday parties at the Grand Hotel in Malmö for family and friends: the slightly down-at-heel bourgeois grandeur of the hotel, the broad staircase, the worn carpets. Speech after speech, in the Swedish tradition. The culmination, every year: a model vintage car made of chocolate, solemnly carried in by two waiters. My uncle broke off the first piece; the car was whisked away and came back broken. Each guest picked a piece in a ritual that seemed almost sacred, such was my uncle's passion for his collection of classic cars.

I write "solemnly carried in by two waiters." But do I really remember how the chocolate car arrived at the table? I thought I did. But when I try to reach the memory, it whites out and vanishes.

*

My mother's brother and his wife had a boat and a summerhouse in the Stockholm archipelago. The boat was anchored off the island, which was reached by a small rowing boat. I remember sitting on the wooden jetty with my siblings and cousins, watching my uncle row out. For some ill-fated reason he decided to stand up. The boat started rocking, then rocked more and more as he tried to control the motion. We laughed, on the jetty. We shouldn't have, but we did: we were easily amused as children. *Jiggle jiggle jiggle*, my mother used to say, mispronouncing the hard *g* of "giggle," and we would laugh even more, rolling on the floor in uncontrolled mirth.

My cousins laughed more cautiously: they knew that the line between *laughing with* and *laughing at* can be crossed by the reaction of the object of fun. My mother didn't mind being laughed at; my uncle did. He shouted in frustration, and finally fell overboard, swimming to shore like an angry seal.

Many years later, my uncle succumbed to dementia with Lewy bodies, a dramatic and fatal disease. He was a civil engineer, the head of Stockholm's traffic planning at the time, and was diagnosed after grinding to a halt in his car in the middle of the road.

Eventually he was moved to a hospital ward for people with incurable dementia. It was a sunny ward with tea dances and cake, my mother said. I suspect that the horror of his dementia may have inclined her to this upbeat narrative of music and dancing, of panoramic windows, of water views, of a new girlfriend (or so he thought), a fellow patient.

My uncle's wife, an architect who had cared for her own infirm parents, and whose brother had died of a brain tumour, was stoic, as were my cousins. I still wonder what their stoicism in the face of those minds, those brains, corroded by tumour and the "gravel" or "sand," the protein Lewy bodies, may have cost them.

My grandmother died of Alzheimer's, or possibly vascular dementia. Strictly speaking, she died with it, not of it—what she actually died of was pneumonia left untreated. *It is better so,* as they say in Sweden. My mother talks about the moment when she realised that her mother no longer recognised her. She still, I think, recognised her son.

Her favourite, as my brother was my mother's favourite.

At the same time—1971—her father was dying of lung cancer. My mother told me only recently that he was eventually moved to a nursing home known, she said, for being "merciful" towards their patients.

"What do you mean, 'merciful,'" I asked.

"Well. They gave him a powder. And that was that." I took in the implication of this.

"Did he know that he was being given a powder?" I slowly repeated the formulation to make sure we both knew what it meant.

"No," she said, looking me in the eye. "He did not."

Was that true? I don't know. Perhaps my mother misremembered. Perhaps there was no powder and no merciful way out for the terminally ill.

. . .

Sometimes it may be that it is better, or easier, to forget. But there is a cost to forgetting, too—a cost for the next generation, trying to make sense of the past. At best, that might mean a lack of hinterland, a paucity of stories. At worst, it can lead to the frozen grief now called *complicated*, marked by a prolonged state of extreme sadness caused by the inability to digest and assimilate what happened.

3

Summer of 2012. It's two months since Eva died, a week after she was found. I am in Sweden, in our summerhouse by the sea. I drift to the window; I look out towards the water, the junipers, the fields of stone. Suddenly I see a brown hare on the cracked stone steps leading up to the house. It tentatively jumps up, step after step, sometimes sitting up, nose twitching. Where is it going?

I stand stock-still, looking at it. Leo, my spaniel, is behind me, eyes level with my calf. He hasn't seen the hare, or sensed its presence. This is what it must be like when we're not here, I think, when this house is locked and still, the earth turning on its axis, spinning into another season.

We had joked, earlier, about the hares. My fascination with them infects the others.

"Mum, we saw the hares boxing!" says Daniel, my son.

"It was more like a dance," says my nephew, looking at me, blue eyes like lamps.

Later, my husband Eric and I are driving, alone. We stop the car on the back drive through the fields. We study the hares, running to and fro. Eric is from South Africa and doesn't know the hares like I do.

"Hare we are," he says, mildly.

"That's neither hare nor there," I respond, automatically.

"Bye-bye, *mein lieber hare*," he sings quietly, keeping up the game I am suddenly too sad to play.

*

The children have gone out. I am, for the first time since it happened, alone in the house.

Eric went to get groceries, and some photographers and journalists who were on the lookout for members of our family spotted him. They took photographs and asked for comments; his nonresponse became a story in the newspapers the next day.

"I am big in Sweden," he said, laughing quietly.

Big in Sweden. Eric is a producer and echoed the joke of his friend the Russian film director Sergei Bodrov: *I am big in Kazakhstan.*

What was that all about? It seemed so funny at the time.

"What is your earliest memory?" Eric asked, to make me think of other things. I thought of the nauseating smell of a chauffeur-driven car, a Mercedes, and the alienation of being in the care of a driver. I thought of the bananas someone fed us to combat nausea. Where were we going? Here, probably. Why the driver? Who knows. One of the two company drivers, I assume, from Tetra Pak, the milk- and juice-packaging company founded by my grandfather, led by my father. He built it up from five employees to some thirty-six thousand people.

. . .

The bliss of summer. We would sing, euphorically, in the car all
the way to our summerhouse:

> *Way way back many centuries ago*
> *not long after the Bible began*
> *Jacob lived in the land of Canaan*
> *a fine example of a family man*
> *Jacob, Jacob and sons*
> *depended on farming to earn their keep*
> *Jacob, Jacob and sons*
> *spent all of his days in the fields with sheep*

Joseph and the Amazing Technicolor Dreamcoat—Lisbet and I
knew it all, every song, and most of *Jesus Christ Superstar*, too.
We knew the Beatles and Tom Lehrer and many Swedish songs.
We sang the mournful *Den Blomstertid Nu Kommer*—"That
Time of Flowers Is Coming"—sung at the end of every sum-
mer term in every school in Sweden and associated with deep
happiness, therefore. We sang *Uti Vår Hage, Där Växa Blåbar*
("In Our Meadow, the Blueberries Grow"); we sang *Kalla Den
Änglamarken* ("Call It the Land of the Angels") and *I Sommarens
Soliga Dagar* ("In the Sunny Days of Summer"); we sang "Sum-
mertime" and "Edelweiss"; Bellman and Bob Dylan; Simon and
Garfunkel and Woody Guthrie.

Did my brother sing, too? I can't remember. Perhaps he did,
a bit.

My brother: straggly brown hair, green eyes, sooty eyelashes. A
touch of something different about him; I am not sure what. He
was a bit unkempt, perhaps—but this was the '60s and '70s after
all. We were all a bit unkempt. Lisbet was pale and gangly, too,

with green eyes. Same brown hair, same green eyes, same dark eyelashes. I was plain, Lisbet was pretty; I was rebellious, she was good. But there wasn't really much in it. Twins and neighbouring countries maintain what Freud termed the narcissism of small differences. We maintained our separation, but people did sometimes mistake us for each other on the street. I could be pretty, too, in a good light. And Lisbet rebelled, in her time. My brother of course was a boy, so he was different. But still, the three of us were made from the same basic ingredients, the same shades of hair and skin, the same kind of minds, the same handicaps, the same talents.

Or did I imagine that?

*

Summer. We threw ourselves into the sea. We threw ourselves into stormy waves. We threw ourselves off the rocks.

We played lawn tennis with soft rubber balls. We pumped them up through a hardened patch of the rubber, with a scary syringe-and-needle pump. We paced out the tennis court on the lawn and marked the boundary corners, flour spilling unevenly.

We staged gymnastics shows on the lawn with our cousins, in Marimekko T-shirts and shorts, in swimming costumes, in our pyjamas. We stood on our hands and descended into bridges; we stood up from the bridges; we stood on our heads; we turned cartwheels.

We cycled to the village. I fell and cut my knee on a sharp stone; the blood coursed down my leg. I was proud of the scar, one of many.

We went crabbing off the stones and brought back buckets of tiny crabs. My father cooked them with dill and we ate them.

They tasted of sea with a lingering aftertaste of sweet dill; a celebration of summer.

One summer my cousin Christina and I kept two of the crabs as pets, dutifully fetching small bucketfuls of seawater to the stone fountain where they lived. Mine was called Lola. They had stones to hide behind and fish to eat.

Eventually we released them back into the sea. We assumed they preferred freedom over captivity, but perhaps they didn't.

The summerhouse was closed for the winter, but we had a weekend house, too, not far from my grandfather's estate farther south. He bred racehorses and kept two stallions, and we had a horse and two ponies there. The mares stood in their large foaling boxes; our ponies were at the end of one wing of the stable.

We called our grandfather Ruben, I suppose because my father did too. If I try I can still hear his voice, though faintly now.

Ruben taught us to play ping-pong and poker; he taught us about mushrooms and species of trees. I remember the smell of his house: carnation soap, geraniums, starched linen napkins, and a hint of dog. We were given pressed tomato juice with Parmesan biscuits before lunch; we ate roast chicken with blackcurrant jelly and finely sliced cucumber in vinegar and sugar. There was a ping-pong table in the basement, an old piano, hollow elephant feet with lids, and hundreds of paperbacks on shelves, an overflow from the library above.

I remember a photograph: he is lying on the lawn wearing a toy Indian feather headdress. My brother, three or four years old, is in his arms, reaching towards the brightly coloured feathers. They are laughing, so intent on each other.

I see in my brother my own son and time shifts and settles.

·   ·   ·

My brother didn't ride. Nor did my mother, after trying my pony, which had originally been hers. Every Friday my father, my sister and I would ride the horses to our own stable, through the melancholy fields of southern Sweden, the fog coming and going, coming and going, past farmhouses with yellow lit-up windows, chained dogs barking, across gravel roads that must now be long since paved, making our way through the woods, one dirt road after another. On Sunday afternoons we would ride them back. Kol, our pointer, ran with the horses.

In the summer, we brought the horses with us to the sea. I groomed them and cared for them; I devised schedules and polished bridles and saddles. I called them and they came for me. I meant good things, especially for my own pony with his sweet itch, his mane and tail rubbed bloody and bald. I put ointment on his wounds; I held his head, which turned heavy in my arms as he dozed.

That heavy head.

In distant summer childhood, we made pretend coffee with dock flowers in our playhouse—a gift from Ruben—which eventually turned derelict. It's gone now.

We played on the swings. I remember my mother on the double swing with my brother, singing, over and over, *I love you and you love me*—how did it end, that song?

We went out in the boat to watch the seals; to picnic on the island. The heady smell of petrol and fried chicken still makes me think of summer and freedom. I would stand next to my tall father at the wheel, jumping each time the boat hit the water, wave after wave, holding on to the wooden frame of the small windscreen. The rougher the better, jumping, jumping, the light 1960s motorboat bouncing from wave to wave.

On the island we read as we ate on the rocks, we played in the clear water, we drank fizzy lemonade in Rigellos, the Tetra Pak rocket-shaped plastic bottle which eventually failed.

I drifted on the common by the sea, back and forth, back and forth. You walked to the left, or you walked to the right. For years I walked, dreaming of spaceships, of abductions. I walked and dreamt; safe, so safe, climbing rocks, jumping from stone to stone.

When summer was over and the time came to return to Lund, the town where we lived, I would swim one last time for the taste of sea on my skin and in my hair; I would sit in the car sucking my salty hair, contemplating school.

Some years ago, Hans gave me the summerhouse next door, which my mother had bought and given to him. He didn't want it.

I love you and you love me. That gift, that house, was how the song ended, or at least one verse of it. My mother tried to keep him here, but couldn't.

*

The ancient common land below our house where the farmers graze their cattle is now designated a nature reserve. It's a ten-mile strip or more of juniper and stone fields between the sea and the ploughed fields above; dry and springy short grass, miniature meadow flowers, and old stone walls. There are bunkers from the war, facing Denmark. There are stone mounds, Bronze Age graves, half a mile from the house. The sun sets in the sea beyond. From the low slabs of rocks at the edge of the sea you look straight into the setting sun. On hot days the air shimmers.

Every summer, the farmers let their heifers out on the common to graze. The cattle wandered back and forth in my childhood, as they still do. Sometimes we forgot to close our gate, and they would get into the garden. Sometimes we were tempted to forget, for the excitement of what happened next. I would hear them first: the dawn clip-clop on the old stone paving outside my window; the heavy breathing of cows. My father, waking up, would place his children in key positions while he moved behind the heifers with his stick. My mother was not amused, but my father, I think, found it as exhilarating as we did.

Our summerhouse was an old fishermen's cottage. My parents are still there, every summer. The house Eric and I stay in now, up above, was designed and built by our neighbour—he was an architect and spent every summer there. He had been married several times and had many children, some of whom were our age. Sometimes they ate with us—my father cooked—and sometimes we watched films at their house. I remember a glorious season of horror: *The Body Snatchers*, *The Fly*, *Them*, *The Creature from the Black Lagoon*, *Jekyll and Hyde*, *Frankenstein*. One night that summer—we must have been about eleven and twelve—my brother ran ahead of me to scare me by a window: a white and ghostly face outside the small cottage where I slept, alone. I screamed, haunted by horror films, by bodies possessed or taken over.

Another time Lisbet and Hans and I were alone in the house, together with some friends. We gradually fell into a panic about vampires, and cut garlic and painted crosses on every window.

Apart from that one night I don't think we were ever alone.

One day followed another. We climbed onto the roof of the guest cottage next to mine and jumped down to the lawn below; climb, jump, climb, jump. In the evenings the stars, constellation after constellation, emerged in the long summer twilight and satellites crossed the sky in a steady pulse. We lay on the roof, watching.

I moved into my tiny cottage with my yellow teddy bear when I was five, to get my own room. I would always wake at three, at sunrise, then fall asleep again. I don't remember being afraid.

My teddy bear seemed half alive when I was a child. Now he is inanimate, propped up on a mantelpiece in London, leaking stuffing. He had a particular smell which I loved, a comforting smell, like a whiff from a live being. There is a faint hint of that smell—synthetic stuffing—around him still; I sniff him sometimes as I pass. I can't have him restored: the smell, all that remains of his life, his spirit, would disappear. He has some old black stitches on his shoulder—my own inexpert stitching. When I broke my collarbone vaulting over the leather horse in gym we had the same fracture.

That leather horse. It was set higher and higher and higher. There was no outcome other than a fall or a refusal. I jumped higher and higher, until I fell and crashed.

Sometimes I lost my teddy for months on end—the summerhouse was closed for the winter, but there was the house in the woods at weekends, and quite a bit of travel, too, and he sometimes got left behind.

I also had a furry seal, small enough to fit into my hand. One year I lost my seal. For months I listlessly searched the attic of our house in Lund, a quiet space spanning the width of the old townhouse. One wall had slatted shelves, weighed down with old copies of *Country Life* and *Krokodil*, the Russian satirical magazine my father read. There were many cupboards and hidden spaces, and an extra attic above, which didn't have a proper floor, only yellow insulation in between the beams. I had read *The Count of Monte Cristo* and *The Three Musketeers* and longed for secret passages. I searched for them behind the tiled stoves in the drawing room and dining room, and in my parents' bedroom. I searched my mother's wardrobe, which connected to my own bedroom via a small internal window, through which a child could crawl. I went down to the cellar, past my father's old golf clubs on the steep staircase into the smell of hot dust from the boiler. I searched for something, what? Some inner solution, perhaps, some explanation to the mystery. But what was the mystery?

There was a cold room in the attic where my mother stored her furs and coats and perishables: crates of mangoes from friends in Pakistan, and flat foreign boxes of chocolates from Tetra Pak customers, which I would gradually eat my way through in secret.

I searched for my seal and I searched for secret passages.

Next to the cold room was a room with two vast freezers. Like deep sarcophagi, they held, for years, the remains of two feral cows my father had shot on my grandfather's estate. Their hides ended up on one of our floors, brown and glossy, and we ate beef stew for years made by our cook from Goa, John Menezes.

Under one of those freezers in the attic I eventually found my dusty seal.

John made beef stew and bread pudding. He made fruit salad and homemade vanilla ice cream, packing the wooden barrel with ice and coarse salt, turning the creaky handle. I cycled home from school in the afternoon, and John would make me coffee with hot milk and sugar, dusted with cinnamon. I would cut two slices of bread and butter them, adding thin slices of cheese. I would prop myself up in bed, and read. Pony books and Astrid Lindgren, Edith Nesbit, Mary Norton, C. S. Lewis, Laura Ingalls Wilder, Tove Jansson, Anne Frank's diary, *Fairytales from Vietnam*, the abbreviated *Thousand and One Nights* for children, Esther Hautzig's *The Endless Steppe*, Tolkien, Katarina Taikon and *Hitty, Her First Hundred Years*.

I painted my old bicycle red. I remember the lovely smell of paint, the bicycle as quasi-animate as my teddy bear, old, stoic, and patient. I cycled slowly north on school mornings, the cathedral bells striking eight. By November the sun would hang like a blood orange in the fog as I cycled past the botanical gardens, up the road where I picked up my best friend Pamela, through the little park by the blocks of flats, then on to the brick-and-tarmac school, the harsh space.

If it was my turn, I would take our dog Kol for a run in Lundagård, the dark and damp university park outside our house, with its tall trees and worn lawns in the shadow of the cathedral. Sometimes Kol would decide to run off to the larger city park, down the length of Södergatan, the main street of town. A certain tilt of the tail and nose to the ground signalled his decision to go. Once he made that decision, only my father could stop him. I read his body language and anxiously ran behind, pretending not to know him, hiding his lead. In the park he would graciously take note of me again, running gleefully across the sunny lawns.

I, too, ran away sometimes, and understood his wish to be free.

*

Back to those summers. I would help my mother hang laundry on the clothesline. The sea wind saturated the sheets and towels; no sheets or towels ever smelled so clean. We took down the dry sheets from the clothesline; my mother held two corners, I held two. We stretched and shook and folded, stretched and shook and folded, again and again.

My father did all the shopping and cooking in the summer; my mother did most of the cleaning and laundry, with our help. He took out the rubbish; we burnt what we could in a rusty barrel he'd shot holes in for ventilation. I remember the fires at night, glowing fragments of newspaper whirling up in the heat. We watched, mesmerised. At times some plastic slipped in, a chemical smell like the smell of plastic on the shop floor of the Tetra Pak factory.

Sometimes I was afraid of the dark. My father, standing with me by the fire, told me that dark was simply the absence of light. Nothing to be afraid of. And such was his authority that I believed him.

Now we are in the summerhouse my brother gave me. The children are on the roof watching the sunset. Eric and I sit below, listening to the sound of their feet as they run, their wild games so similar to our games when I was young, in this same house, and in my parents' house next door. There's the same TV room, the same black tar-paper roof, the same pungent and heady smell of rotting seaweed from the beach below. We cooked and ate the crabs then; now we release them back into the sea. And the world of layered smells we lived in—the washing, the ironing, the smell in the greengrocer and the fishmonger—seems more muted now, just as the euphoria of arrival, of summer and freedom, has become tempered.

Perhaps there can be no euphoria without a degree of suffering; no feeling of freedom without its absence.

It warps your sense of time, taking children back to the world you grew up in. It is bewildering. Everything is the same; nothing is the same.

Occasionally I bump into friends from that lost world, the world I slipped away from thirty-five years ago. It's like nothing has changed; no one seems to have aged or changed much. *Hey, how are you?* they say. *And Lisbet? And HK?* as my brother was then known. *And Hans and Märit?* they ask, remembering my parents, too.

We have a ghost presence here.

I am writing this in the playroom, filled with our old toys and books. There are hundreds of names and telephone numbers written on the bare pine walls, most of them scribbled down by Sten, the architect who built this house and spent his summers here. This was his office. I find my own old number in London—he might have written it down to give to his son, I suppose.

Sten and his wife would come for drinks with my parents—dry martinis with olives, or champagne. Cheese noodles and peanuts, his wife in pink lipstick and 1970s tan; my mother in her old Marimekko cotton dresses that lasted for decades. They would sit on the wooden steps looking out over the common and the sea, watching the sunset, watching for a green flash, watching for the black rabbit—there was always one.

The black rabbits are gone now.

Looking at the wall I can see all our children's names, too; they have signed the wall each year we have been here.

On a shelf is a little house my sister Lisbet built in school woodworking class, and a wooden car, also hers. Amongst the books—our childhood books—I find my Pony Club calendar from 1973. There's my name in my eleven-year-old signature, and Jappo, the name of my pony, in 1970s bubble letters. I sit down to read it, remembering every article, every piece of horse advice and pony lore, every black-and-white photograph of girls with their ponies.

I was eleven in 1973. Hans turned ten, Lisbet thirteen. There were three years and six days between them. I was born twenty months after Lisbet, and Hans was born sixteen months after me.

My mother put all those mementos in this house for my brother.

*

One of the Granta editors gives me Anne Carson's luminous and painful book *Nox* about her lost brother, who eventually died in Copenhagen. I read it with fascination. They had nothing in common, Carson writes. Her brother called her *pinhead* or *professor*; there was no common ground, and yet he left a void behind him.

The three of us, by contrast, were so similar, as though mixing my mother with my father could make only this one combination, more or less, of height, of green eyes, of brown hair.

And if we were all the same, is the implication that what my brother did, I might have done, too?

Perhaps I should rephrase that: is the implication that what *happened to* my brother might have happened to me, too?

I read Jane Austen; he read Charles Bukowski. I turned left; he turned right.

The summer ends and we return to England.

Melancholy London, melancholy Knightsbridge.

There is Mr. Chow. My parents used to take us there forty years ago to eat drunken fish.

There is the discount carpet store, advertising its sale, 80 percent off, year after year, season after season.

There is High and Mighty, closed now. My father used to buy shirts there.

There is Please Mum, where I bought my son's cream suit for my second wedding, to Eric. Daniel was five, and looked like a mini-mafioso in his suit, with my brother's dark eyelashes, my brother's serious watchfulness.

I notice that I am hesitant to begin the story. I write around it.

Hans and Eva met in rehab, in their mid-twenties.

They got engaged.

They got married in 1992.

Her family happy, our family happy, after so many years of addiction, of anxiety, of unhappiness, of blame, of denial, of disappearances.

This, finally, was recovery.

The wedding was a celebration of that, as much as a celebration of love and the founding of a new family.

By 1999 Hans and Eva had three small children. Their youngest son was not yet born. They had a house in London, a house in Barbados, many cars and paintings, many things. Headed notepaper and invitations to this and that and philanthropy and house parties and lunches and dinners.

Were they happy? I think so. Happy enough.

But perhaps I didn't pay enough attention.

*

I have lunch with my parents. My father sleeps; my mother and I walk through the house, looking at paintings, looking at photographs, looking at her collection of glass. "To tell you the truth I am bored with it all," she says. We meander on through her memories, through her house. In a drawer she finds some photographs of the grandchildren when they were small; the school photographs I used to send to the family every year.

We look at the pictures. I remember the uniforms. Breakfasts on dark mornings, a pile of kitbags gathered by the door. Five pairs of school shoes lined up by the coats; the cricket bats; the tennis rackets; the homework diaries; the crumpled bits of paper children bring home from school.

It seems so long ago.

I stand with my mother in front of a cabinet as she absentmindedly opens drawers. She finds a wedding photograph of Hans and Eva, bleached by the sun. Eva is looking down, smiling; Hans looks straight at the camera, holding his head high, a happy smile.

And under it, in a silver frame, is a photograph of me and Eva, sitting on the steps outside my parents' house, in front of the old orangery. Behind us is a blurry child, throwing her head up to look at the sky, but I can't see who it is. What year is it? I search for clues. I am wearing jeans and a cotton jacket I still have. My ex-husband's watch: that's a clue. A bracelet; a gift from him.

My hair is so dark. I look young, and happy. Eva looks happy, too. What is she wearing? A white cardigan, a skirt? I can't quite see. Bare legs, tanned. The grass is green; I am guessing it's early summer, June. Eva looks American, blond hair flying in the wind, confident and strong.

There we sit, leaning slightly towards each other as people do for photographs. My arms clasp my knees; I squint into the sun. Eva's hands are under her legs, holding up her skirt, her bare knees touching, one foot slightly over the other.

The silver frame acts as a mirror; it catches my glasses, my face, my greying hair.

After Eva died, I stopped going to the hairdresser; I cut my hair myself for a year. I would take a strand of hair between my fingers, feel the split ends, and cut the strand off, a little pile of hair forming on the side of the basin. Eva would not have approved of that, had she been sober, and alive. She would have rightly diagnosed it as a sign of distress and made me stop, because the counsellors at the rehab were right: she did have the gift of persuasion.

She might even have taken me to her own hairdresser. She might have sat with me, sipping cappuccino and discussing hair, in that parallel universe, normal life.

The photograph may or may not have been before the millennium New Year. I remember the nervous questions: would the Internet collapse through jamming date functions, would everything grind to a halt—flights, banks, cities, governments? No one knew.

Hans and Eva went to a party, and drank a glass of champagne, to celebrate. Or maybe several glasses, for the first time (or maybe not the first time) since recovery. The date functions didn't jam and the airplanes didn't fall from the sky, but our world was fractured that night, by those glasses of champagne.

4

Over the next few years the signs of addiction accumulated, though we were not as yet aware of the extent of Hans's relapse. We worried about Eva in particular, and we worried about the children. In June 2004, I wrote to Eva to suggest that she go to rehab. She didn't respond. Of course she knew that rehab doesn't work so well if you have done it many times before. You know the vocabulary and the shortcuts, the pretty prayers, the glib sayings. If you have seen it all before, perhaps you see through it.

I think of those many letters that I wrote, those useless sentences. I don't know what she made of them, and I don't know what they made of me.

Looking back, I can see that I didn't understand how hard it was for Eva. Her layers and layers of acting out and acting in tricked me; the pose and the authenticity, those refractions of addiction where the pain is sometimes the authentic thing and sometimes the pose; where hard laughter is sometimes the authentic thing and sometimes the pose. There seemed to be empty spaces in Eva's body and mind itching for drugs and for freedom, cavities that might have been filled with contentment, or work, or family love, that subtle connection between parents and children, and their children in turn, that animal thing which is about feeling better, and safer, when *the loved ones* are in the room.

The knowledge that you will be protected and that you belong: the primitive function of love.

I watch Asif Kapadia's documentary film *Amy*, about Amy Winehouse. I recognise the contrast between the distress of her friends and the detachment of Amy's own narrative, that facile pose which is part of addiction.

I am moved by the grief of Amy's friends. I know what they are doing, grasping at the dull straws of recovery-speak, those clichés that are all we have. But most of all I am haunted by the selfies taken in the weeks and days before Amy died: those dark observant eyes watching her own face, so thin, so bony. The camera as mirror. Her heart worn out by cocaine; by bulimia; by alcohol. Those eyes are so searching, almost scientific, coldly neutral as mirrored eyes always are. There is no message—she is observing herself.

I wonder if she believed in the danger she was in.

She played with death, obviously. Perhaps death was her faith, a belief in the *what then*, the thrilling unknown. I think of the romantic enactments of the European tradition—nihilism and Russian roulette; war and heroism; Goethe's young Werther triggering an epidemic of suicide; the suffering in jazz; the rebellion in music.

I don't think Eva quite believed in her own mortality, even though she often referred to it in her long emails. But those references always struck a slightly false note, as though they were part of some longer game between us; a game we knew was not quite real. Her rebel days were over, in any case. She was no longer young, no longer the party girl she had been. Now there was so much order all around her; so many things; such delicate or suffocating networks of obligations. She wanted out, I think.

The line between addiction and recovery is so fine, and so vast: a tiny step, a movement in a dance; a huge commitment.

In Hans and Eva's house the bedroom was the private sphere, the locked room, the drug space. The drawing room on the floor below was a model of bourgeois order. The bedroom contained the addiction; the rest of the house felt like a front for the recovery they, or we, had hoped for, the family life they, or we, had wanted—a Potemkin façade of affluence and stability.

After the children came to live with us in May 2007, the life went out of the house. The staff waited; the house waited. That clean and empty kitchen, those subzero fridges, that big garage: so easy to inhabit a house like that again, if you know how. So easy to step back into that old order.

And so easy to relapse, too, if you know how. Addiction is a culture; addiction takes knowledge, like any other way of life. You have to know how to operate in that culture, how to trade, what things cost, what doctors will help, how to keep safe.

Before they relapsed, Hans and Eva had stopped going to 12-step meetings. They let go of solidarity with other addicts; they became funders of addiction causes instead, flattered and praised, like all philanthropists. Perhaps in fact that was the beginning of the relapse, that lapse of solidarity, that seduction of philanthropy.

I also don't think that Eva believed in rehab any longer, at least for herself. I did, because there was nothing else, really. What else can you urge on a drug addict, if not rehab? And what else can you do, if you are not urging, planning, pleading, asking?

Chaos theory teaches us that the effects of small events—the beat of a butterfly's wings—are not just unknown, they are actually unknowable, because the elements involved are too numerous and too varied. The specific course of addiction, too, is difficult to predict. People who are no more than mildly addicted sometimes succumb; people who seem lost do sometimes recover. There is always hope. And that hope is both wonderful and terrifying, because you search so desperately for what might help. Hope sucks you in. If you never give up hope, you are locked into the addiction.

That is why Families Anonymous, the 12-step fellowship for family members of drug addicts, asks its members to recognise the limits of what they can do. The first step reads:

> *We admitted we were powerless over drugs and other people's lives—that our lives had become unmanageable.*

You can walk away from the addicts—*other people's lives*. But you can't walk away from their children.

I read my letter from June 2004 again. Those useless sentences.

"I am writing this because I have been so worried about you for the last few months. I know it may not help, but I do feel I have to do something."

"Eva, you are very ill. I don't know what it is you are taking, but I suspect it's a cocktail of all kinds of different things. You desperately need help, and I would very much like to help you."

"I wonder if you are aware of how everyone in the family, and all your friends, are extremely concerned about you."

"I think you are in a frightening state where anything could happen—the illness, as we call it, has come back."

"The problem is that the descent into rock bottom is so long if you live the kind of life we do. Propped up by nannies and staff one could go on in a twilight existence of alcohol and pills for years. There are enough posh and sordid doctors in London to prescribe you with whatever you want."

"Please know that I am on your side—I know it's not easy for you."

"You were so strong in your recovery, Eva—I remember that. So articulate about the process, so active in helping others gain access to the kinds of treatments you had, so centered and so compassionate."

"When I said to you you should be an addiction counsellor I wasn't joking, or flattering you—you would be wonderful at it."

"So please please don't think I see this as a moral failing on your part. And know, finally, that I am there for you, on your side. Whatever you need, whatever I can do, I will help you with."

"I don't want to invade your privacy, but neither do I want to see you slide downhill while everybody looks on, saying nothing. It—life, I suppose—doesn't have to be like this."

"With very much love."

. . .

Grasping at the dull straws of recovery-speak.

Who did I become over the course of those hundreds of letters, texts, emails, conference calls, and conversations? A guardian; a team with my sister, with our husbands. A guardian and a guard, perhaps. Individual letters and random conversations became a process; the process gathered momentum.

I ponder that first step.

We admitted we were powerless over drugs and other people's lives— that our lives had become unmanageable.

I became a prisoner of hope, and a prisoner of addiction.
    But if I hadn't engaged, who would I then have become?

Judging by this particular letter, by the summer of 2004 we didn't realise that Hans had relapsed, too. But sickness was in the air: a kind of hovering malaise.
    In September of that year, Hans came to visit us in Sussex with the children. It was very hot. In the evening the children devised and put on five or six short plays for us, morbid and enticing little horror stories. Eric, Hans, and I sat at the kitchen table, clapping and laughing. The next day, my diary records, was hot and hazy. Hans was nebulously ill.
    I feel sick, like Hans, I'd written.
    I read that, and think about denial.
    I feel sick, like Hans.
    Why didn't I see it?
    And why didn't I see it before, when Hans was living in my Islington flat in the late 1980s? We were in our mid-twenties. Hans had left one of his many rehabs. My mother thought

it would be a good idea if he stayed with me for a while. He relapsed straightaway, and none of the signs of drugs spoke to me: the plates of rotting food, his reclusion and passivity, the sweet and rancid smell of heroin smoke.

And then he left.

Why didn't I see it before that, when he came back from India in 1983? He was twenty. His hip bones jutted out, his upper arms were thinner than his wrists, he had cut his own hair. He was in hospital, eating bagfuls of wine gums, hooked up to a drip. He had a stomach parasite, he claimed.

Perhaps he did.

The doctors and nurses looked on and said nothing.

My sister Lisbet, who read this book in manuscript, wrote a comment in the margin at this point. "Why would we see it," she wrote. "What did we know about mental illness, or tropical diseases, or drug addiction."

It occurs to me that this is true. When Hans came to stay with me in Islington, I had started work on my PhD. I had a life—the beginnings of an independent life, the beginnings of a career. How did we, as a family, conceive of addiction, I wonder now. How could it have been left to me to deal with a young person with a potentially fatal emotional illness; a condition so existentially threatening, and one which we knew so very little about? Did we think this was going to be a passing phase? Did we think he would sort himself out?

He had no help. I had no help. We lived in my beautiful though somewhat dilapidated maisonette on Liverpool Road in Islington. After some months I asked him to leave.

He didn't leave. Perhaps he couldn't. Perhaps he didn't have the energy or the impetus. Perhaps he had nowhere to go.

By the time I asked him to go, he had stopped washing. By the time I asked him to go, I still hadn't understood that this was about drugs, even though I was fully aware that he had just come out of a rehab. Such was the power of my denial.

He didn't leave when I asked, but he remained in his room afterwards. It was a small room, that second bedroom, a child's bedroom, I guess, at some point. He stayed in that room like a neglected child, dirty and dishevelled, with a distracted sister for a mother.

The defining condition of being a sibling is this: you see through each other. You get it. You think you get it. You are more impatient than maternal. But how spectacularly wrong I got it.

And maybe it was just a good place for him to stay, a convenience. Perhaps that's what I never understood, with my excess of emotion, my sentimental empathy, my existential angst.

I thought he was still my little brother, a kid with a sweet milk moustache, chocolate powder under dirty fingernails. I felt so guilty about his small room, about asking him to leave because he was not cleaning his room again, not doing the dishes, again. I didn't see that he had grown up.

And maybe he hadn't. In some ways he was still that messy child. But the chocolate powder had turned into heroin, a dark and sticky substance under his fingernails.

*

When we were children, during term time, Hans would watch television for hours: Czechoslovakian cartoons, Astrid Lindgren adaptations, *M*A*S*H*, *Starsky & Hutch*, punctuated with scenes from Swedish TV studios with their bland presenters, potted plants on low brown tables, or sometimes just a clock, ticking, ticking, ticking.

This was in our townhouse in Lund, on the top floor. On the wall was a climbing frame. We climbed and hung; we played don't-touch-the-floor, stretching from sofa to table to climbing frame to chairs. We played horses on the stiff back cushions on our '60s sofa, striped in brown and beige and cream.

My brother and I dripped wax from burning candles onto cartoons in the attic to make wax prints, a red toy bucket of water next to us. Donald Duck and Mickey Mouse; how nice it was to drip the melting candle wax, flame oozing, wax stiffening and turning white, drawing up the image from the print on the page underneath.

Our Dutch au pair, the daughter of a professor friend of the family, picked mushrooms with us in the woods; we sat at the rough stone table on the lawn of our weekend house cleaning them. My parents were away, but some friends came by and found us there, placidly brushing grass and earth from the poisonous mushrooms we were about to cook and eat for lunch.

Random memories; hidden dangers.

School was a prison, we had to endure it, but then we were free. At weekends Hans and I played poker and five hundred with multiple decks of cards; I made up new rules when we got bored. We threw our cards down with a certain panache; we made bets with matches; we aimed, and failed, to learn the cool shuffle. But in town Hans was more quiet than me, more likely to watch television, while I taught Kol, our dog, to run by my bicycle—nose high sniffing the air, tail in a jaunty arc—and Lisbet read in the town library.

Who was he meant to be, this quiet child?

Lisbet and I became academics because my mother had

been an academic. We gave it up, as she gave it up. We were not conscious of her as a role model, but of course she was: we map our lives with reference to our parents and to our culture.

But who could my brother model himself on? He couldn't become my father in a meritocratic society like Sweden.

Heroin is a very loving drug, someone tells me. I can believe that. "A precious substance whose unadvertised charm was love," Victor Lodato wrote about crystal meth in his short story "Jack, July." The love of the drug, the safety of the drug, replace, some therapists believe, parental love and safety. But what if that absence of love is linked to an inherent inability to receive and process love, an emotional lack, a born or acquired deficit? Born and acquired, perhaps.

My brother stayed with me through the summer, that time in my Islington flat in the late 1980s. Then, one day in August or September, he was suddenly gone.

I had no idea where he was, and heard nothing. His small room haunted me. I cleaned it, but it was still a rebuke, as though I had imprisoned him there. And like a neglected city after a revolution, I shut down, bit by bit. A button fell off my coat; I didn't replace it. My underwear turned grey; my socks developed holes; my shoes were old. Newspapers blew across the road; the lorries thundered up towards Holloway and the north; I went for long and aimless walks.

I was sad, but I was able to carry on with my work. I saw friends. I called my parents. Lisbet sent thick manila envelopes of newspaper cuttings about this or that, matters of interest, from America; she was at Harvard then.

We waited.

.   .   .

In February the following year my mother drove down to the village in Sussex to see about a cheque that didn't seem right. This sentence looks so normal on the page, but in fact my mother rarely, if ever, went to the village. The idea that she would personally go and see about a cheque that didn't seem right is so out of character that her decision to do so seems almost psychic. Because there, in the bank, was my brother, waiting in line. He had come over from Amsterdam to get cash; he was living there. And my mother took him home.

My mother is from the north. Mysticism lingered there: some women were healers and could stem blood, even over primitive phone lines—the ability to stop bleeding was a useful knack in the deep forests of northern Sweden, where forestry workers sometimes had terrible accidents. My grandmother was of Finnish extraction, descended from the seventeenth-century Finns who were given poor marshland to settle the Swedish middle north. Their villages were accessible only in winter, when the marshes froze. The inhabitants were almost self-sufficient— early on they even made their own guns from marsh iron.

But Sweden was changing. My grandmother wanted to study chemistry at Uppsala University, but then her father died, and with his death her chance of a university education died, too. For a while she taught in the remote Finnish villages in the marshy badlands. These were rough places. She bought a gun and made sure that the men noticed her daily target practice. Later she told stories of men stabbed for cheating at cards; of whole families dying of tuberculosis; of the hunger in the north during the First World War.

My grandmother was formed by mysticism and modernism, one tugging at the other. And on the day long ago—it must have been in the 1930s or 1940s—when her brother swallowed all the sleeping pills the nurses had counted out for him night after night in hospital, she sensed his decision long before the hospital called.

*

In Amsterdam, my brother had put himself on methadone to try to wean himself off heroin. The methadone was giving him blackouts: he was calm, but absent. My mother got him into another rehab, a rural one this time. She went to see him there every Sunday, as did I. We took part in the weekly family meeting, when family members visited their addicts and alcoholics, their anorexic girls and compulsive eaters, their sex addicts and compulsive gamblers, and shared their anxiety and grief and anger. The addicts had to take it: family members had taken it for years, walking on eggshells, cautiously setting new boundaries that were broken again and again, and now they were dishing it out. We were purged at the meetings, before walking back into our own lives.

My brother got better there, and as he got better, I got worse. This time my depression was no longer like a bleak postrevolutionary dilapidation. Now it was a palpable presence, possessing me. A cold claw held me by the throat. This malevolent being plotted to kill me, to throw me off the roof, to stab me. It held me captive where I was.

My academic work ground to a halt, and my professor called me. I stalled on the telephone; couldn't place that so very familiar voice, a kind voice. Someone who was obviously trying to help me, but who? My deeply preoccupied mind failed to recognise him for several minutes, or perhaps seconds.

My cousin, whom I liked, came for dinner with his wife; I had forgotten and panicked when they rang the doorbell. I took them to the Indian restaurant around the corner; a great effort. I got through it, but only just.

Everything was a cover-up. Why was it so important to cover up my distress? I don't know—but there it is. It's easy to express vulnerability when you are strong, and almost impossible when you are not.

My power of association withered—those constant echoes of the healthy mind. You see a tree that reminds you of a childhood garden; and that game, that wild game of running from garden to garden through the town; the freedom and excitement that reminds you of America; a warm sun, a Camel cigarette; a random crab bake in New Orleans; a dark sky in Colorado; that film, that film . . . What was that?

The depressed mind doesn't echo. It is mute.

I correct myself: my depressed mind didn't echo.

What do I know about the minds of others.

Lisbet kept sending those thick manila envelopes with cuttings; my mother and I kept meeting, every Sunday, for those cathartic family meetings. "And how are you, Sigrid?" the counsellors would say, looking at me thoughtfully. "This must be tough for you." I cried and cried. That was a relief.

In between, I could barely leave the house.

Eventually the counsellors became sufficiently concerned about my depression to suggest that I come in as a family member for residential treatment. Sometimes family members become so entangled in the addiction that they need help. This rehab occasionally took in such people and treated them much as they treated the addicts, in the same groups. My brother had to leave first, of course, for a halfway house in Weston-super-Mare. He left, and there was no bed, but one would come up in the summer, they said, or maybe later. I was on the waiting list.

And then one quiet evening in early summer, I got a knife and cut long and shallow stripes in my arm. Drops of blood sprung up, strings of red pearls. I stood in the kitchen and cut patterns and stripes, my cat weaving in and out between my legs, miaowing, weaving, pressing herself against me. I remember considering the question of whether her reaction was an expression of concern or whether she was excited by the smell of blood.

And then I broke. I cried until I couldn't breathe. I rang the rehab, and a bed was found for me the next day.

I was the first patient, they said, that they had ever put on antidepressants; but the pills—this was still, at least in Britain, the pre-Prozac era—made me faint, so I stopped taking them. My brother was in Weston and wrote me a supportive letter of breezy recovery-speak. But I was not an addict, and I was by temperament and training a sceptic. There was a limit to what the place could do for me. Being around other people in a therapeutic environment helped, of course, though I felt the craving pull of knives—perhaps I was an addict after all? I knew that I was safer in the rehab than I would have been at home. And when the psychologist evaluated the psychometric tests new patients took and found that my profile matched that of an average addict—*I enjoy watching fires*, was one of the questions, *yes or no?*—he concluded that I was an addict in denial. Probably an alcoholic, since I didn't take drugs.

I didn't really care. I was happy to be called anything as long as I could stay. But the false diagnosis undermined the logic of the treatment, which didn't make sense anymore. When I read out my Life Story it was rejected by the group on the grounds of denial—not enough, if any, alcohol-related "damages" were in it: instances of neglect and harm to myself and others. In fact I didn't drink much, and I never had drunk much. I was pliable in the beginning, then I started to withdraw my admission of alcoholism. That was a sign of sanity, but of course the counsellors and the group didn't see it like that.

I finally left when one of the members of the group was asked to stand on her head in the middle of the circle. She was said not to follow the group's advice and had been threatened with expulsion. The "advice" was unfathomable—abstract and contradictory. I don't think any of us could have summed it up. When she said she would do *anything* to be allowed to stay, one of the patients drawled that he wanted her to stand on her head. The counsellors did nothing; the woman, who was not young, stood on her head, briefly.

The next day she was asked to leave anyway. That act of humiliation had been all for nothing.

I called a taxi, which took me to the station. I took the train back to London, after more than two months in that country house rehab, outings limited to one walk a week, sometimes not even that, and Sunday visits to a small stone church in the middle of a wood.

It was late summer. London was relatively empty, yet it felt shockingly busy and aggressive. None of the strangers I saw on the street knew where I had been. I dodged the crowds awkwardly; chatted to the taxi-driver so he wouldn't sense my disorientation. We pulled up in front of the house in Islington; I walked up the steep bare staircase to the first floor. There was my cat, narrowing her eyes, quietly noting my arrival. There were my friends who had been house-sitting. They greeted me cheerfully; we went to the kitchen. And there, on a cutting board, next to some innocent carrots and leeks, was the knife I had used to cut myself. One of my friends, still talking, picked it up.

Time stood still for a split second. Then I bent down to my cat. Life, my life, resumed.

*

Rehabs are closed worlds and strange things happen there. I found it difficult to talk about it to people who hadn't experienced it. They were often embarrassed, as though I had found religion or joined a cult. When I think about it now, I am struck by how "recovery" was really linked with getting to know people, with moving so quickly from the status of stranger to the intimacy of the group. People came in unknown and messed up: addicts with a swagger and empty eyes; bulimics humble and self-effacing; anorexics calmly controlling, surveying the room; alcoholics with their loud and raspy voices, their narrative knack; troubled family members smiling nervously. We were all imprinted on the group like newborn ducklings. We had a schedule of meetings of various kinds; we walked around and around the garden; we sat and talked by the vegetable plot; people smoked, endlessly.

Sundays were unsettling. Now I could see how hard the family meetings were from the other side, and how the counsellors framed the meeting to protect us. Sunday evenings were subdued and serious, with a weekly open 12-step meeting— anyone could come but mostly the participants were former patients and those amongst the counsellors who themselves were in recovery.

And knowing the fallibility of the group method and the limitations of the treatment, I still believed in rehab for Hans and Eva. It's like believing in school for children: there are few alternatives.

I gradually got better, and resumed my PhD. But I was still fractured, still given to overidentifying with the fates and lives of others. It hadn't just been my brother. Earlier on, that flat in Islington had harboured a friend with severe anorexia, followed by another one who had become an alcoholic. I was trying to help. I was well intentioned, but my boundaries were so fragile.

After the rehab I tried to get by. I moved to another flat; I covered up how distressed I was and hid my panic attacks—time and time again I thought I was dying, my mouth numb, my mind faint with anxiety.

A few years later, in 1993, I went to Estonia, to a tired modernist village in a former border protection zone. I lived there for a year, conducting fieldwork for my PhD on the process of de-collectivisation. The state of the country mirrored my own internal state: there was little or no welfare and no viable security forces. People grappled with the effect of censorship and Stalinist repression—Estonia was marked by history and by loss of history.

It was, however, a profoundly peaceful place. I slowly cured myself by taking long walks, by reading, and, most of all, by my research and writing. I was gripped by curiosity about that strange place and that national condition. I wrote myself out of the aftermath of depression.

But look behind the door and it's there.

I have some aural and visual migraine symptoms, migraine without pain. But the pain is there, a grey shadow waiting. I just don't feel it. I don't want to feel for it, because I'm afraid it might come. My depression and anxiety are the same.

And it did of course come back in the twenty-odd years after I left Estonia. But by then I had built up my own culture of defence, my own internal state. Now I know too much to be dragged down into it. I trick my mind, I jump over the crevices, but I make it.

Eric stands on the other side calling me. He seems to see value and strength in me. But even he doesn't quite understand how, when the depression comes back, it feels like reality, like the grey and sensible light of day after a heady night. Memory and identity leach out; my confidence seems like a pose, a high, a drunken illusion; my true self a plain and bony figure in possession of a canny realistic mind. A tired mind.

"Who do you think you are," Eric says kindly, in a mock Swedish accent, green eyes half closed, studying me. He says it to remind me that I am Swedish and that I must consider the effect of the national ethos I grew up with—*Who do you think you are* is part of my bone marrow. *Don't think you are better than anyone else.* He reminds me of the tricky reality of depression—part culture and part nature. He says it to remind me that what feels so real, that depressive default setting, doesn't have to be true anymore.

We discuss whether depression and addiction are genetic or environmental. I am writing a memoir of addiction, a history: that seems to imply a belief in external causes. But in fact I believe that all states are a combination of genetic, emotional, and cultural conditions. Privileging one over the other seems to me the wrong way of looking at it—the factors involved are infinite and varied, more like colours in a painting than fixed notes in a composition. Genes are one: there may be a genetic fracture in us, and in my mother, too, and her grandfather, and others—one or many mutations, weaving in and out of the generations. I don't suppose my depression was caused by my brother's acts—it may have been another sibling thing between us, my depression, his addiction; a similar emotional deficiency, or a similar emotional state.

And then again there is such a thing as depressive realism: studies have found that people who are depressed tend to be more realistic than others about their own abilities, and about their social standing in a group. Cheerfulness and resilience are mutations, too. Our acute understanding of the nature of life—we live, we suffer, we die—might become unbearable without those rose-tinted glasses; without our inclination to happiness and optimism. Resilience helps us to survive.

We can't easily grasp or explain the complexities of our emotional lives. Describing the taste of wine is hard enough; putting words to emotions much harder. We use coded expressions for how we feel, but in fact we feel through the body, not the mind: the rising heat and quick energy of anger; the faintness of anxiety; the exhaustion of depression; the levitating flight of happiness; the gravitational force of desire.

And what about the other sensations, the physical symptoms that have no names, at least known to me? Every so often, my mouth tastes of ash; the taste plagues me. I am sometimes enveloped in passing smells—of rot, of honey—that might be phantom, might be real.

We exist in body and brain; the meeting between the two is consciousness and mind. Nothing that we feel or think is wholly physical or wholly imaginary—the brain interprets the body, and the body interprets the brain. But we must still try to describe, and understand. As David Grossman said, putting words to emotions is what makes us human. It differentiates us from the animal world. Creating a narrative aids understanding, and not understanding negative emotions can be dangerous. If you fail to make sense of depression, it can turn you into something other than what you are, or what you were. It can turn you into someone drawing pearls of blood from wrist to elbow like blood-red jewelry; like lace; like strings of lights.

5

In May 2005 we went to Scotland for a week. At the last minute I had to travel up on the sleeper—I had a cold and couldn't fly with Eric and Daniel. *It's hot outside; the train is oddly dismal,* I wrote in my diary.

I wasn't thinking about Hans and Eva. I was writing, and reading old diary notes about Daniel, flicking from page to page and from year to year, missing him even though I had only just left him and would see him again the next day. The nostalgia of motherhood: he was eight then, the early years already behind us, memories echoing as though from the bottom of a dry well. I had written down some of the things he had said when he was very young and I read them again on that train to Scotland.

"Mummy, when you have a bug, do you have a fly in your tummy?"

"Mummy, I had such a strong dream last night. I dreamt that my soul was pulled out of my nose and it was blue."

"Mummy, I am sick."
"Where does it hurt?"

"Everywhere. Everywhere in my whole body except my heart. My heart is OK."

Motherlove. *I love you and you love me.*

I was in Paris recently to launch an issue of *Granta* at Shakespeare and Company, the English-language bookshop. The next day I walked along the river, to the botanical and zoological gardens. It was still early, and the yak was dozing in the zoo, alone in her small paddock. She woke up and looked at me thoughtfully, heavy horns, rags of winter fur, a blond fringe. Her stable was a gesture at the Tibetan or maybe Mongolian vernacular, though not for her benefit, of course. My back ached; I felt so stiff, so old.

I wandered over to the *singerie*. A L'Hoest's monkey, a mother, sat with a baby. The baby's long arms were wrapped tightly around his mummy, he was nestling in her lap, tiny black hands clutching soft fur. The mother was eating; the mother was resting. She was deeply peaceful. Behind her sat an older child, aimless, a little restless. Once that child too was wrapped tightly in warm clean fur. Now she sat behind her mother, still so safe.

I thought of Harry Harlow's rhesus monkeys. In a series of experiments in the 1950s, Harlow, an American psychologist, removed baby monkeys from their mothers and offered them a choice between a cloth "mother" and a wire one. The wire mother gave the children milk, but they still preferred the soft cloth mother, the mother they could cling to. The cloth mother punished the babies with metal spikes and pushed them away; they still tried to cling to her. Harlow caused such pain to prove something about the universal nature of love. He was searching, innocent and mystified, for the invisible essence of love which most people can sense intuitively, even between animals.

Motherlove, babylove. I walked back to my hotel, my attic room. I was tired. I stretched my back, I lay down on my bed, heavy like a yak.

*

We have a new puppy, a silky spaniel. I lie on the sofa, he lies on my stomach, he wriggles and exposes his pink tummy, he gazes at me intently with black eyes. What does he see? Suddenly he hears a sound, a gurgle, and stands on tippy-toes, then jumps like a fox catching voles in the snow, thrusting his nose into my stomach. I laugh, I hug him. But what am I to him, if it's possible that my body is also a drift of snow or leaves, concealing voles? He knows me, but it is possible also that something live and good and biteable is hidden inside me and that he can penetrate the surface of the body-snow.

My puppy fawns on me; he rolls over, he submits, he bites, he bites. I pick him up, I kiss the top of his head; he throws his head up casually and licks me on the lips, once, briefly. That licking on the mouth is a feeding reflex for puppies—canines feed their young with regurgitated food—but it is also an expression of love.

What was the blood on my arm to my cat? Maybe the truth about thought—human, animal—is that it is so rarely just one thing. My affectionate old cat, a beaten-up kitten found on the road, may have been excited about the smell of blood and at the same time anxious about the smell of blood. Sometimes we miss the nuances, the infinity of causality, the shades of colour on the canvas: real life.

Text and speech are only representations of real life.

*

In the summer of 2006, Eva almost died from endocarditis, a heart infection, probably caused by dirty needles. Her heart was damaged, and she needed an operation to replace one of the valves and a pacemaker to regulate the heartbeat. Hans, deep in his own addiction, hadn't noticed how ill she was, and neither, I think, had she.

The pacemaker formed a tight square under the skin below her collarbone; she made fun of it and carried on. I remember standing with her in front of a mirror at some charity event. She powdered her emaciated face and the skin over her pacemaker, laughing. She was so thin.

"It's just not funny anymore," someone said to me later.

But was it ever funny?

After that summer our side of the family staged an intervention for both of them. Everything was prepared: two rehab places had been arranged; the transport was ready. We met outside Hans and Eva's house in London.

We sat down. Hans listened patiently as I read our intervention letter, but Eva stormed out of the house, incensed. Eric went after her to try and persuade her to come back, but she wouldn't stop, walking quickly up the King's Road.

The idea that we had confronted her just as she was recovering from her heart operation came up again and again afterwards. It was as though we had hit her as she walked out of the hospital door; kicked her when she was down; stamped on her head. The fact that we were trying to help was no longer part of her narrative—in the beginning she had sometimes acknowledged that we *meant well*. That was over now.

Hans telephoned her, but she wouldn't come back. We could hear his end of the conversation. "Well, but they are right about some things," he said, reasonably. She argued with that; he listened silently. In the end Hans went to Osea Island rehab in the Thames Estuary, and Eva stayed behind. And because their relationship was a folie à deux of mutually enforcing addiction, a powerful normalisation of the not-normal, her denial endangered him as much as it endangered her.

Hans only stayed at Osea Island for a few days. He came in with a supply of heroin and was obviously in a bad way. The staff, following new legislation about protecting children, were obliged to contact social services. From that autumn on, the social workers were involved, and a series of events unfolded which culminated in a custody case and Hans and Eva's four children coming to live with us in May 2007.

I read through the paragraph above and I see how abbreviated it is. I have filing cabinets stuffed full of legal documents and court orders. I can't bear to look at the papers. I don't even know where they are, since the storeroom in Sussex where I kept the filing cabinets is now the downstairs kitchen of the playbarn, and the builders—or someone—must have put the cabinets somewhere else. I think I know where they may be, but I don't know where the keys are.

It only occurs to me now how strange this not-knowing is.

Or perhaps not so strange. In those cabinets are all the sad and sordid details redacted from this book.

Je veux dormir! wrote Baudelaire in his poem "Le Léthé." I lock the cabinets, I lose the keys, I want to sleep, and to forget. Instead I write, fighting sleep.

I struggle to remember. What was that thing, that time, the time we tried to save Hans and Eva . . .

Where are the keys?

In the autumn of 2006 Hans and Eva deteriorated, but they still let us see the children—later on they banned us even from that. The two youngest came to visit us in London one weekend. As I was driving them home we passed my stepdaughter Natasha, then sixteen, on the street and stopped to say hello.

As we drove on, my youngest nephew, then five, said, "I am thinking of something, but I mustn't say it."

"What are you thinking about?"

"She knows." He prodded his sister.

"What are you two thinking about?"

"Does Natasha have a mummy?"

"Yes, she does, and she lives with her mummy."

"But who would she live with if her mummy died?"

"Well, she would come and live with us."

"And who would she live with if you died?"

"She would . . . live with Lisbet."

"And who would she live with if Lisbet died?"

And so on, until every family member and every family connection had died, and everyone in the world had died, and until every dog in the world had died, and my stepdaughter was alone in the universe.

Who would she live with then?

*

I think Hans went to seven rehabs in 2006 and 2007—Osea Island was one of many. Amy Winehouse was there, too, along the way. "A fucking little island in the middle of fucking nowhere," someone says ironically in *Amy*. She is there with her friends; they are sitting around brushing hair, smoking, giggling.

Osea Island rehab closed down when it was revealed that its director had lied about his credentials.

But still, when Hans left after a few days, the staff did call social services.

That was good.

*

In the summer of 2015 Cecil, the soon-to-be-famous Zimbabwean lion, was killed by an American dentist. Everyone was talking about Cecil. "There is one rule for celebrity lions and one rule for the rest of us," someone said indignantly on the radio. I laughed in my car, alone, driving through London.

I had started writing this book, and woke up night after night worrying about it, imagining the ugly Swedish headlines:

HEIRESS SIGRID RAUSING TELLS STORY OF BROTHER'S
ADDICTION

RAUSING PALME MURDER ALLEGATION DENIED

SIGRID RAUSING ON HER BROTHER: "HE KNEW THEN
THAT SHE WAS DEAD"

RAUSING FAMILY SECRETS

HANS RAUSING DID NOT KILL OLOF PALME, SAYS DAUGHTER

Can a book about this story ever be framed by anything other than tabloid headlines?

I had a dream about walking into a café in Copenhagen. No one knows who I am: this is a relief. On a menu blackboard was the line: RAUSING PAID TOO MUCH. I was criticised for paying my own kidnap ransom. The ransom—*too much*—would inevitably support the extremist cause. In the dream I was conscious of sadness.

There is a real link between Copenhagen and kidnapping: more than thirty years ago the Danish police discovered a terrorist plot to kidnap one of my cousins. A random car crash led them to a flat full of weapons—the group, Danish radicals who had become affiliated with the PFLP, the Popular Front for the Liberation of Palestine, specialised in robbing military weapons depots. The police also found a dossier: a detailed plan of the proposed kidnapping. I never saw it, but I heard that it involved a cage; a boat; a hut in Norway. The cage was to be dropped into the sea if they were followed.

This haunted me for years.

It still haunts me.

Before that, there were other kidnap threats. I remember policemen and new alarm systems, loud sirens forever going off in the still forest of our weekend house.

The daughter of someone my parents knew in Germany joined the Baader-Meinhof Group. Another man was shot dead by his own stepdaughter—she too had been radicalised and joined the terrorists.

How many times did we sit through meetings with security companies, scenario-casting kidnaps? How many times did we have to rehearse and memorise sequences of telephone calls; imagine the negotiations? How many times were we given the message to stay under the radar; never speak to journalists; vary all routines; never resist?

My grandfather Ruben had lived in Rome since the early 1970s. After one of his Italian neighbours was kidnapped, Ruben moved to Switzerland, to Lausanne, to fog drifting over Lake Geneva; a town of banks, shoe shops, and misshapen fetuses in glass jars in the town museum.

That was many years ago, before the addiction, before the first headlines, and long before Eva's death.

Eventually the newspaper headlines about drugs began; the floodlights clunked on one by one. We stood frozen in a vast and empty arena, we looked around.

The powerful old patriarchy that ruled the family was dead or faltering; the company was sold; we were on our own.

The nature of privilege: what it means and what it doesn't mean. Pleasure and pain, security and risk, private comforts, glamour and envy.

You walk a little apart, always.

Power. A familial police state. I was, and am, uneasy about power, which made dealing with Hans and Eva's addiction harder than it might have been. I was uncomfortable with the unwitting panopticon we had constructed: the power base of lawyers, security consultants, addiction consultants and family networks. My guilt nagged at me; I was like a nervous dog staring at its own reflection in dark windows.

But I never doubted our intentions. We tried to help Hans and Eva. That help, however, was interpreted as an exercise of power; an oppressive force; a colonising impulse; a familial takeover. Hans and Eva alternated between denying that anything was wrong and blaming us for whatever was wrong—this, I imagine, will be familiar to most people who have had to deal with addiction. We also came to be familiar with the unlimited-love versus the tough-love position, and how families divide into hawks and doves. The doves see the hawks as harsh and unloving; the hawks see the doves as enabling and codependent. Each side secretly or openly blames the other for the decline of the addict. The hawk-dove continuum is not unique to addicted families, of course, but the divisions can become especially bitter because family entanglement is part of the disease of addiction.

Disagreements are so interesting. We flit from discourse to discourse, from cultural tradition to cultural tradition, whatever gives us the better advantage in the moment. Our minds are formed by all the layers of history, all the strands of culture, all the conversations, codes and triggers that we know: culture accumulates, as much as it changes. And at this point in history there are so many accumulated models—cultural and literary and scientific—so many different lenses through which to understand ourselves and the world, each one refracting and reverberating through the others. There is no metadiscourse anymore, there is no certainty, and there is no dominating system of thought. What you say in the context of psychoanalysis in terms of desire or a dream or anger is not what you can say in the context of everyday life. Shifting the context is a strategy of arguments, of the tabloids, and of the courtroom. Those are the realms of attack and defence.

Understanding, and forgiveness, are associated with the idea that in some contexts certain acts may seem, or even may be, "normal" or at least understandable, whilst in others they are not. "May seem" if we believe in absolute ethical values; "may be" if we are true relativists.

I am now an editor, but I was trained as a social anthropologist, and I will probably always lean towards cultural relativism. Anthropologists are dedicated to context; to making sense of culture in its own terms. But contemporary conversations shift between relativism and absolute values; between exploring the unknown territories of the psyche and tabloid truths; between genuinely *trying to understand* and relying on simple and judgemental rules of right and wrong.

The nature of addiction weaves in and out of these conversations and these paradigms. Nothing is certain. Is the addict born or made? Is addiction a genetic mutation; a psychological condition; a culture of rebellion? Are addicts victims or perpetrators? Addicts destroy families—perhaps by seeking so desperately that which they missed, or believe they missed, as small children: the safety of parental love? Do addicts reject love by becoming unlovable? Or do they destroy families blindly, incidentally, indifferently, overcome by cravings, numbed by drugs?

The addict doesn't care. But could the vast indifference of addicts to the pain of others perhaps also reflect their perception of others' indifference to their own pain? Or do addicts self-medicate because they are in fact more acutely sensitive to pain than the rest of us, as some neuroscientists argue?

. . .

I believe that addicts are born in the sense that the child carries a biological kernel of emotional dysfunction, which in certain conditions can grow into an addictive syndrome. But we all spin narratives from unfolding time, and those narratives are also true. Those stories become our lives. The addict is born and the addict is made. As we all are.

Perhaps what I am trying to say is that I got trapped in a web of uncertainty, which haunts me still. I fumble in the dark.

I am not alone of course. We all fumble in the dark.

"The chicken is a little dry and/or you've ruined my life," writes Ben Lerner in one of his poems.

Suddenly I am laughing.

6

In the spring of 2013 I was onstage at the Charleston literary festival in Sussex, moderating an event with authors Patrick McGrath and Olivia Laing about the relationship between creativity, madness and alcoholism. My mother sat in the audience, her long sleek hair in a bun, smiling benignly and only slightly ironically. She nodded at me, willing me on. It was a year after Eva died, and my brother was still in court-mandated care.

A woman from the audience asked a question. We seemed to be implying, she said, that addiction is genetic or at least innate, whereas of course the real cause is a lack of security in early childhood. She knew this as a treating psychotherapist, she added. I looked straight at my mother as the therapist spoke, feeling a wave of anger on her behalf. She had to endure decades of my brother's addiction to be condemned again in this cosy marquee, the cows lowing outside, the promise of the South Downs and the sea beyond. But she looked back at me so calmly I wondered if she had even heard the question.

My mother was a child once. She lay in the snow with a broken leg and the other children left her behind, thinking her attention-seeking (of course she had intellectual aspirations, even then, when her main inspiration was still a cheap edition of *How to Be a Japanese Samurai*).

I guess my mother's Samurai ethos stood her in good stead in the snow and the subsequent months in the women's ward in hospital, her leg in traction, surrounded by cases of infectious disease and blood-poisoning.

My father was a child once, before his mother's illness and death.

She watches over me as I write, her face so gentle. She was certainly ill when this photograph was taken.

I will not judge anyone. And science, less judgemental than popular culture, bears me out.

DSM-5, the latest edition of the American Psychiatric Association *Diagnostic and Statistical Manual of Mental Disorders*, reckons that 40 to 60 percent of the risk of alcoholism is genetic and adds that any given gene is likely to account for only 1 to 2 percent of that. The genes involved are many and varied, in other words, but enough studies have been done to conclusively establish the heritability of alcoholism.

The *DSM-5* arguments for the genetic component of opiate addiction are perhaps a little less compelling:

> The risk for opiate use disorder can be related to individual, family, peer, and social environmental factors, but within these domains, genetic factors play a particularly important role both directly and indirectly. For instance, impulsivity and novelty-seeking are individual temperaments that relate to the propensity to develop a substance use disorder but may themselves be genetically determined. Peer factors may relate to genetic pre-

disposition in terms of how an individual selects his or her environment.

Psychiatrist and addiction expert Markus Heilig has argued in a recent book that all addictive disorders are moderately to highly heritable. He estimates that some 50 to 70 percent of any single addiction is caused by an inherited component. Free will and environment, particularly growing up in poverty, exposure to violence, and limited education, make up the rest of the risk factors. He, like the authors of *DSM-5*, believes that addiction is associated with impulsivity and a poor ability to delay gratification.

There have been many studies on the capacity to delay gratification. The most famous one was conducted at Stanford University in the early 1960s—the so-called marshmallow test. Psychologist Walter Mischel tested a group of children who attended the Bing Nursery School at the university. The children, who were aged four to six, were placed on a chair by a table in an otherwise empty room. They were shown a treat and given the choice of either eating it or getting two treats instead, if they waited for fifteen minutes on their own.

Some of the children were filmed. On the table was a bell to call the researcher back into the room, and the treat itself, a marshmallow (or a pretzel or an Oreo cookie) on a small plate.

I watch the footage: the children fidget as children do when they are supposed to stay on a chair; they stare as though hypnotised at the marshmallow; they make faces at it; they surreptitiously lick or gnaw on it. It's mesmerising but also painful to watch: I want to step through the screen and through time to be with them, those children, who are now older than I am. I imagine that some of them might have eaten the marshmallow just in order to draw the experiment, and the enforced isolation, to an end. But perhaps it makes no difference whether the child is resisting the marshmallow or resisting an easy end to boredom and loneliness—either would take self-discipline, and either would be correlated with age, which indeed turned out to be a strong factor in the ability to resist.

But isn't it odd that if the children were adults, the sanest choice would in fact be to eat the single treat and end the experiment? Time is precious; boredom is bad; social interaction is healthier than isolation. Delaying would be seen as neurotic; an inordinate time sacrifice for an insignificant award, analysed, perhaps, in terms of excessive submission and obedience, a depressive lack of agency. But for very young children, the same behaviour is interpreted as a positive capacity to delay gratification. We posit that the marshmallow is a symbol of everything worth waiting for: all the rewards that come with patience and discipline. But surely a marshmallow is just a marshmallow? Even the children must have known that.

But as the Stanford children grew up, they were tracked, and strong correlations with the original results were said to emerge in adolescence. SAT scores turned out to be higher for delayers, and ratings by parents and teachers on social competence were higher, too. And when the cohort of marshmallow children were followed up again, aged thirty-two, delayers were less fat; and they also, apparently, used less cocaine.

The idea that poor impulse control is linked to drug addiction is by now embedded in popular consciousness. It is hard, reading the original research, to tell what the tests actually show—how far the delay time was correlated with age; how much the subsequent SAT test scores did in fact differ, and how many of the "impulsive" kids were overweight or used cocaine, or both. The papers are dense and require a sophisticated knowledge of statistics. The effects seem to be small, though they are still significant—but of course one of the difficulties of translating science to popular science is that the term "significant" has a different meaning in the world of statistics than in common speech. In statistics it only indicates a variation in the data (of any magnitude) that is not random. Mischel himself in fact cautioned against overinterpreting the data linking the capacity of preschool children to delay gratification to adolescent and adult outcomes.

More important, Mischel soon concluded that willpower and impulse control were not, in fact, entirely innate. "The ability to voluntarily delay immediate gratification, to tolerate self-imposed delays of reward, is at the core of most philosophical concepts of 'willpower' and their parallel psychological concept of 'ego strength,'" he wrote in 1973. But the ability to defer gratification could, he argued, be taught:

> After many false starts it occurred to us, at last, that our young subjects really might not be basically different from the rest of us and hence were capable of following instructions—even instructions to think about marshmallows, or pretzels, or fun things that might distract them. Indeed we soon found that our subjects even at age three and four could easily give us vivid examples and elaborations about endless things that made them feel happy, like finding lady bugs, or swinging on a swing with Mommy pushing, or dancing at a birthday party. And we in turn instructed them to think about those fun things while they sat waiting for their marshmallows.

He developed this thinking in later papers. Current theories, he and a coauthor wrote in 2002, whether psychoanalytic, behaviourist, or genetic, ignore people's capacity for positive change. *Akrasia*, the ancient Greek term for deficiency of will, could be overcome by training. If marshmallow children were told to think of the pretzels as "little logs," or of the marshmallows as "puffy clouds," delay time could be increased by up to thirteen minutes. If the children had toys to play with, delay time was extended too. When the children were told to think "fun thoughts" ("If you want to, while you're waiting, you can think about Mommy pushing you on a swing"), delay time was extended for as long as when they were given toys to play with.

*

I think of my mother sitting on that double swing with my brother, singing, over and over: *I love you and you love me.*

Did it help him to remember that? Could he have been patiently taught, like Mischel's experimental subjects, to delay gratification and curb his cravings?

We grew up in the era of the original marshmallow experiments, the 1960s, with its fine line between neglect and freedom. We were not taught to understand and moderate our feelings, or to share them. Were we neglected, or were we free? It's hard to say. Perhaps the occasional holes in our socks and the tangles in our hair, our freedom to run a bath in the evening or not, to do our homework or not, was a form of liberation—the price we paid for being free.

Freedom was the Zeitgeist. In the spring of 1969 the students occupied a university building opposite our Montessori nursery school, where we tied shoelaces in frames (so mysteriously hard for me; so seemingly easy for others); where we were lined up at break to race to the swings, to swing so high. We watched the students on the roof from the swings; we heard the slogans through crackly loudspeakers.

It was such a peaceful town, otherwise. We walked to Montessori through quiet streets. We walked in line to the bakery to buy a plain bun for morning break, or maybe afternoon break, or maybe lunch. If you carried on, you reached Domus, the co-op, and the town market square. If you walked back towards our house, you passed the pet shop and Folkets Hus on the other side, the trade union cultural centre.

For a long time it felt like fifteen or twenty years ago. Now it feels like a hundred years ago.

We thought we were so modern. But then so did our parents, and so did their parents before them.

The students burnt their caps, those traditional symbols of graduating from high school. *Palme and Geijer, Nixon's lackeys*, they shouted then, or maybe later—the slogan rhymes in Swedish and doesn't translate well, but you get the gist. Olof Palme, Social Democratic prime minister, and Arne Geijer, the head of the trade union, lackeys of Nixon. In Lund, young men refused to do military service and were prosecuted; students demonstrated in the cathedral against a South African visit.

Those were radical days, and Olof Palme adopted some of the causes as his own, chiefly the demonstrations against the Vietnam War (leading to the American ambassador being recalled in May 1968) and anti-apartheid activism.

My mother had been a Social Democrat when she met my father. She travelled to political conferences in Yugoslavia and other places; she believed in progress and equality. She taught at the university, worked on her PhD, and didn't expect to get married. Then one day she was introduced to my father, and was married within three months.

Her radicalism was transformed into liberalism, maybe because she was influenced by my charismatic grandfather, a dedicated liberal who believed that true progress was industrial. But she never quite became domesticated. On weekends she made us breakfast and Sunday night pancakes. Other than that, this is someone who never cooked, and whose own mother's loss of a university education was associated with a quiet sense of defeat. This is someone who had held on to a student room long after she was entitled to one; who told my father that she would marry him but she would never cook. He didn't mind—he loved her, and he loved cooking. It became part of the story of who they were.

Everyone was busy. My father was building up the company, with my mother's help—"Doing well by doing good" was the slogan. Clean milk for schoolchildren in Kenya and India. Clean milk for everyone.

My mother's grandfather came from a well-off landowning family from Jämtland, one of the northern counties bordering Norway. He was an alcoholic, who drank and gambled until the family eventually shipped him off to an estate on the island of Gotland, where he died young. Not much money remained. He left two sons, one of whom was illegitimate. When my great-grandmother discovered this boy's existence, she adopted him and brought him up as her own. That boy, too, became an alcoholic (his son in turn became a great man, but that's another story). "I think of my grandfather," my mother would say, in reference to my brother. That genetic thread running through us, weaving in and out of generations.

Motherlove. I don't think love was lacking. Perhaps my mother didn't quite understand, or accept, the principles of motherhood. But who amongst us has a firm existential idea of that mysterious concept—what it is and what it means?

Women get blamed. Remember the now debunked notion of "refrigerator mothers," the idea that autism is caused by emotionally distant parents, mothers in particular? Psychologist Leo Kanner came up with that idea in the 1940s (and later distanced himself from it). Bruno Bettelheim made it a household concept.

Every woman has to invent herself, as Simone de Beauvoir said.

*

The neurological research carries on. RISKY RATS SHINE LIGHT ON GAMBLERS, *The International New York Times* reported in March 2016. Karl Deisseroth, a neuroscientist and psychiatrist, had found that certain neurons in rats' brains determined behaviour. Rather like Mischel's marshmallow children, rats given a choice between a steady flow of sugar or an alternating trickle and flood divide into those who go for thrift and those who go for bust, defined as risk-averse and risk-prone individuals. Professor Deisseroth showed that if part of the risky rats' brains were stimulated with light, they could be turned risk averse. He was also able to dampen risk aversion with a drug for Parkinson's disease, reversing the process.

"We know from other work that this is all relevant to human addiction and gambling," Dr. Trevor Robbins, chair of the Department of Psychology in Cambridge, commented. I wonder, though, about framing rats' appetite for sugar in terms of risk, rather than in terms of stability, or intelligence, or metabolism. Once you use that term you are in the field of addiction: *risk*, like *impulse control*, or *deferred gratification*, is not a neutral word.

And why is it that we problematise the behaviour of the risky rats, rather than the behaviour of the thrifty rats? I genuinely wonder which is the mutated state, the thrifty or the risky one, but I sense my own sibling syndrome in the question too. Am I the risk-averse rat pressing the lever of modest returns; hiding in the wood shavings wondering why all the attention is on the risky rat? Am I the self-righteous sibling reluctant to join the celebration of the brother, the one *who once was lost and now is found*?

We recognise the type: he was risky, that prodigal son. But surely our view of risk, and our propensity for risk, is historically and culturally constituted, too. In London we like it in wartime and bull markets. In bear markets, especially post-crash, we value caution more.

Different drugs have different effects, and addicts have marked preferences. I associate cocaine with a certain manic quality, which makes sense of the idea of "risk taking" as a gauge to measure that addiction. But opiate addicts may not be risk prone at all. What if their existential condition, in fact, is that they can't face the risks of life without the honeyed prop of drugs?

But even as I write, I sense that I am just speculating.

I used to joke with my sister and her first husband about an imaginary journal, *The Intuitive Scientist*, edited by speculative non-scientists like us.

That was fun. That was a long time ago. Our minds were still spinning patterns from random thoughts.

.   .   .

Professor Heilig has done a TED Talk and blogs about compassion for addicts. The insular cortex, the region of the brain associated with emotions, shows more activity in the brains of addicted people exposed to painful images than in the brains of nonaddicted people, he says. He deduces that addicts feel pain, their own and others', more acutely than other people, and that they probably self-medicate to dull the pain. Even if we don't find new medicines, he hopes to be able to change judgemental and excluding attitudes and policies.

I'm moved by Heilig's humane approach, but what does it mean in practice? Maintenance programs, I suppose—most commonly methadone or other man-made substitutes. There are many studies and metastudies showing that regular methadone stabilises mood and reduces HIV infection and criminal behaviour. That has to be good, and preferable to the dangerous cycle of short stints in prison or treatment followed by relapses and potential overdoses due to the loss of physical habituation.

Professor Heilig wants us all to hug an addict. I, too, believe in the power of love, but stock protestations of love may be meaningless to addicts, and equally meaningless to family members. Proclamations of love can feel artificial, especially if there is underlying anger. Small falsehoods, when perceived—and we are all masters of perception, while retaining the false belief that our own flattery or praise is less transparent—can lead to anxiety, alienation, or tolerant contempt, and anxious family members can confuse expressing love with a suspension of judgement, leading to collusion and enabling. Isn't it better for addicts to be heard and understood than to be "loved"?

Winston, the hero of George Orwell's *Nineteen Eighty-Four*, endures episode after episode of terrible pain while O'Brien, his torturer, reads his mind, accurately predicting his internal responses to mind-control techniques. They both understand that the aim is not to gain information—there is no information to be gained—but to break Winston's mind. And like Harry Harlow's rhesus monkeys frantically clinging to their punitive cloth mothers, Winston, now drugged, clings to his internal vision of O'Brien's wise and ugly face. The man, despite everything, is someone he can talk to. "Perhaps," he thinks, trying to understand this surge of affection, "one did not want to be loved so much as to be understood."

What chilling ambiguity Orwell draped around that innocuous phrase. The fact that it's true—one probably would prefer being understood, a meeting of minds, to being loved—doesn't alter the fact that at this stage all of Winston's thoughts, including this meditation on love, are a predictable result of the torture.

There are no easy answers. There is as fine a line between medicine and poison as there is between therapy and interrogation. Every good model—tough love, limitless love—has a shadow, and every good quality or principle can become distorted and oppressive.

But perhaps a definition of hell is a lack of trust—it makes for a cold world, even if you are not an addict. Maybe that's what faith and love (known cures for addiction) are all about—a leap into the dark. A decision to trust.

Addiction comes in many forms and degrees. At worst, you are locked into a loop: most drugs, opiates in particular, create a hunger which can be relieved only by more drugs. People turn secretive; their cores fracture. When the illness is severe, the addict, trusting no one, is trapped.

Unlike most drugs, opiates are physically addicting. But even heroin cravings are partly emotional. What other force could create such intense longing? Adding emotions to neurol-

ogy is like adding gravity to physics—it's an elusive and mysterious force, but without it the theories don't make sense. But since
blame and mistrust are such intrinsic components of addiction,
there is danger in identifying causes; danger in creating narratives of unhappiness which might explain the emotional part
of the addiction but could also feed it. That's why 12-step programs steer away from causation.

Addiction is an emotional disease, and while methadone seems
to reduce harm by tempering craving, that indescribably intense
and hungry longing for a substance that transports you from one
emotional state to another, it's not a cure—it's a policy solution
of instant harm reduction, both to the addict and to families and
society. Methadone is the weapon of realpolitik, not idealism.

You can argue the causes of addiction and the efficacy of treatment models every which way. I believe that addiction is a
spectrum condition—and that we are all on the spectrum. The
neurological model, based on the binary distinction between
neurotypical and addictive brains, one or the other, doesn't seem
to me to recognise that. The genetic model of course is less
binary, since the view now is that so many genes are involved,
one way or another. Each one plays a part. And I imagine it's
likely that some mutations give protection against addiction,
rather than the other way around.

There is the factor of time, too: what we are and what we
become, in essence, can change.

*

Eric and I went to Tate Britain to see the Frank Auerbach show
a year or so ago. Afterwards we happened to wander into an

exhibition, just one room, on Art and Alcohol. I stood in front of a large painting titled *The Last Day in the Old Home* by Robert Braithwaite Martineau (1862). Eric was tired and sat down; he leant his heavy head on his hands and closed his eyes. I knew I should go to him, but I couldn't leave this painting, this vibrant tableau of a stately home, soon to be sold, a dissolute father holding up a glass of champagne to the light, his son, no more than ten or so, standing by him, with his own glass of champagne. The unhappy mother reaches out towards her son, a useless timid gesture.

The father's expression reminded me of the husband-villain Arthur Huntingdon in Anne Brontë's 1848 novel, *The Tenant of Wildfell Hall*. Huntingdon, too, drank and tried to draw his young son into drinking; he had an affair; he was absent and cruel; he was morally bankrupt.

The painting glistens; the sumptuous dark hall and everything in it must be sold. The man is a gambler, the summary states. Hardham Court is to be sold, ". . . thanks to the irresponsible behaviour of a feckless spendthrift." The text details the visual clues, strangely only mentioning the champagne as a sign that father and son prefer "to live for the moment." How reluctant we are to be moralistic about alcohol, even when a father gives his young son a glass of champagne, in an exhibition dedicated to the theme of art and alcohol.

The epic painting *The Worship of Bacchus* by George Cruikshank, completed in 1862, is there, too, a vast canvas at the centre of which is a man, drunk, dancing on a stone pedestal which is engraved with an epitaph: SACRIFICED AT THE SHRINE OF BACCHUS, FATHER, MOTHER, SISTER, BROTHER, WIFE, CHILDREN, PROPERTY, FRIENDS, BODY AND MIND. In the background stand the eminent punitive institutions of the day—the asylum, the workhouse, the house of correction, and more—and in the foreground are scenes of drinking, of violence, of degradation.

Every generation reinvents its narratives and its drugs. Remember Edie Sedgwick, Andy Warhol's heiress friend, who died aged twenty-eight of an overdose? How they crashed and burnt, those Sedgwick children. Edie was anorexic and spent time in numerous mental hospitals. One brother committed suicide; another died in a motorcycle crash that Edie believed may have been suicide, too.

Edie met Warhol in 1965. He took to her immediately and made a film in which she starred: *Poor Little Rich Girl*. She eventually broke with him and moved to the Chelsea Hotel, where she hung out with Bob Dylan and others, took drugs, and was hospitalised again and again, in between getting "vitamin shots" laced with speed and acid from a celebrity doctor.

Edie eventually married a fellow patient, Michael Post. She stopped using for a bit, then relapsed. In the end she died of a barbiturate overdose, in bed, next to her sleeping husband. "I gave her the 'meds,' and she started falling to sleep really fast," he says in Jean Stein and George Plimpton's book, *Edie: An American Biography:*

Her breathing was bad—it sounded like there was a big hole in her lungs . . . this sort of flopping, rough noise. She was such a cigarette fiend. It was a fixation with Edie to feel the heaviness of smoke in her lungs. She wanted to stop when she was thirty. That night it sounded so bad that I thought of waking her up and telling her that if she didn't stop tomorrow I was going to give her a spanking or something.

The next morning he touched her shoulder and she was cold.

Andy Warhol's other superstar, the wealthy and troubled Brigid Berlin, taped the conversation in which she told him about Edie's death. Writer and film critic Bruce Williamson heard the tape. *When*, Andy asked, and how could she *do* a thing like that, and would *he*—Michael Post—inherit all the money?

Brigid told him there was no money. Well, what have *you* been doing, Andy said then.

And Brigid started talking about her dentist.

They fetishised that slightly camp indifference, of course, Andy Warhol and his followers.

If you don't feel pain, is it still there; a ghost pain? If you cause others pain and feel no remorse, do you then have ghost guilt, an unconscious shadow staining your mind?

I contemplate this, talking to my psychoanalyst on the telephone. I sit in our guest bedroom; I have locked the door. This is a relief. I sometimes sit in the sky-blue armchair by the window; sometimes I stand up and lie down on the bed, cautiously, so that he won't hear me move.

He knows my caution and says, many times, that this is my time. I can do what I like. I don't have to turn up at his office, lie on his couch, stare at the dots on the ceiling, line up the dots to draw dismal squares and shapes in my mind.

"People do all kinds of things," he says. "Sometimes they make telephone calls they can't make on their own. Sometimes they read letters out loud."

I am sitting on my chair, talking, when I hear a muted exclamation on the line. "It's all right, it's all right" I hear my psychoanalyst say gently to someone else. My mind flashes to the story of a friend doing family therapy with his wife and small children at the Tavistock Institute in London, and the shocking discovery that there were fifteen students sitting behind a one-way mirror observing the family interaction "for training purposes." The session, my friend found out, had been secretly taped on video, too.

My analyst laughs a little. "It's my dog," he says. "She's dreaming."

"It's all right, darling, go back to sleep," he continues, with such gentleness, and I don't know why but I think of Leo, my old dog, now dead—"put to sleep," as the expression goes. He would doze on my lap in Sussex after the children left for school in the mornings. I would make another cup of coffee and lie on the sofa in the kitchen reading, with Leo sleeping on me. When he got too old to jump up, he would stand with his two front paws on the sofa, locking his eyes with mine, and I would lift him up. When he got too old to do even that, he would walk stiffly back and forth. I'd be reading, my right hand dangling to the floor, my cup on the back of the sofa leaning against the wall. Leo would walk himself between my hand and the sofa, so that my hand, resting, would stroke him automatically.

He walked up; he turned; he walked down; he turned, back and forth, back and forth. Sometimes his head buffed my hand. Buffy Sainte-Marie, we called him, between ourselves, teasing him behind his back. Buffy Buffy. I would sit on the back steps and hug him; wave goodbye to the children with his paw.

7

During the twelve years of Hans and Eva's relapse I had a recurring fantasy of kidnapping my brother and taking him to some remote place, slowly detoxing him there, bringing him back to life. I thought about who could help me; I thought about doctors; I thought about locks. I felt guilt about the fantasy, but at the same time I was also guiltily aware that it was my brother I fantasised about kidnapping, not Eva. Guilt for not doing enough and guilt for doing too much, guilt for fantasies of kidnap, guilt for the lack of fantasies of kidnap.

I doubt in any case that it would have worked. Addicts need to detox, but they need to reshape and rebuild the architecture of their psyches, too. It turns out I am not alone in this fantasy, though: other people have told me that they too have fantasised about kidnapping their addict. Addiction can seem like membership in a cult or a form of possession: the people you love are in there somewhere, bewitched like C. S. Lewis's Prince Rilian, who was kept in an underground cave he thought of as the whole world. If you starve the demon of drugs, the former person might emerge.

But perhaps in fact it is the family members who are possessed. Their own accounts of addiction tend to be existentially painful, while addicts' accounts are often curiously casual. Family members are on constant red alert; they are obsessed by the addiction; they go to such lengths to rescue, to save, to help. There is an addiction model for this—codependence. The addiction to the addiction. The absorption into other people's lives and fates, at the expense of one's own.

After Hans's stay at Osea Island, the social workers got involved. I liked them, but by spring of 2007 it was clear that there was little they could do, and that Hans and Eva were getting worse. The social workers became increasingly concerned, until the fateful day in April 2007 when they told Lisbet and me that unless we took measures to remove the children, they would do so themselves. And that if they did take such a measure, it was most likely that the four children would be split up.

The court case.

I am reluctant to go back to those awful days.

The thought of our judge comforts me. Judge Barron was a woman in her sixties, occasionally impatient, obviously intelligent, and slightly intimidating. "Yes, yes, I understand that," she would say impatiently, "but what I am trying to get at is . . ." *Yes, yes, I understand that* became another thing Eric and I would say to each other, a code, a reference, a shared history.

Fragments of memory. Lisbet on the cold floor of the restroom in the family court, sobbing. She is weeping so much she can't breathe; I hold her.

The theatre of giving evidence. Lawyers try to trap you by shifting the discourse. How hard it is, always, to remain focused on the real issue, not to be drawn into the shifting discourses. We had to prove that we had nothing against Hans and Eva. We had to prove that we were not taking the children for our own gain.

In a case like this, everyone is under scrutiny, as of course they must be.

There were many interim hearings between the first one in May 2007 and the last, a two-and-a-half-week trial in February 2008. Hans and Eva arrived in court hours late every morning or even in the afternoon. Hans would be slumped forward, eyes half closed. Eva would fidget, increasingly restless, looking up at the clock on the wall, crossing and uncrossing her legs. Then she'd abruptly leave. Some time later she'd be back, swaying, slowly making her way to her seat, dreamily looking around her. Judge Barron observed, weary and astute. I think she knew that this would not end well. But we didn't. We didn't understand that every addiction case is the same dismal story.

Everyone in the room had seen it all before, except us.

Those years of failed hope. By the autumn of 2007 we had realised that Hans and Eva were not going to rehab, as we'd hoped they would, following the first hearing, when the children were temporarily placed with us. We had imagined that they would stay with us over the summer, and that by autumn they'd be back with their parents.

I wrote in one of my letters to Hans and Eva about seeing Sean Penn's film *Into the Wild*, a young man's journey into the wilderness of Alaska based on Jon Krakauer's book about Christopher McCandless. In the end McCandless can't get out: the river has risen. Trapped, and fatally poisoned by mistaking one plant for another, he dies, emaciated, on an abandoned old bus, his temporary home in the wild. He had left his family, his rather ordinarily oppressive family, or perhaps slightly more so: it seems he couldn't bear them anymore. Or perhaps he just wanted to be free, and join that lonely cult of freedom, the American wild.

I think of my brother's wild trip, when he was younger than McCandless: the trans-Siberian railway, through China, through India, to Goa, to heroin. Heroin was the end, the final destination. But heroin was also an accident. He and his friends might never have met those girls on the beach in Goa.

What would have happened then?

I don't know.

Some families are overprotective. Others, like ours, take a secret pride in the wild.

The glory of late-night horror films, running through the night, the wind, the salty wind.

I wrote to Hans and Eva that I imagined that they, too, had gone into the wild. McCandless left his family for nature, for Tolstoy and Thoreau. Hans and Eva left for drugs.

"I can't follow you there," I wrote.

No one could. Perhaps that was the point.

*

The children were with us from May 2007.

They were all so young. The youngest, aged six, sat on my shoulders on a walk. He held on to my head, then pinched my shoulder, quite hard. "Ouch," I said. "That hurt."

"I do want to hurt you a little bit," he said. I squeezed his feet. His life at home was over.

Not that we knew that then.

·   ·   ·

And then suddenly they were all teenagers, talking by text, in code. I arranged to meet Daniel by the cathedral near his school:

"K c u btw r u driving me back with S"

"Yes. Teo is meeting me off the train and we all go back together. Xx"

"K tht will be gd see you soon xx"

That's how it goes.

Time stretches and condenses.

When I look at my emails—archived by year, each file full of correspondence about Hans and Eva—it seems extraordinary that there was time for anything other than their addiction, and yet there was so much time then. We lived in the countryside. There was working time and ordinary time, dinners and breakfasts, school runs and homework, *The Simpsons* and popcorn, hot chocolate and bonfires, rabbits and dogs.

Everything that had previously been a bit ad hoc, with one child, now had to be systematic. Five children make a little school, a herd, a flock, falling in predictable and unpredictable directions, always in movement like clouds of starlings in the sky.

I was nervous about accidents and painted a sign for the drive on an old piece of wood: SLOW CHILDREN, surrounded by garlands of leaves, flowers, a sun. We hammered the sign to a stick and stuck it down in the heavy clay. "Slow children" amused the children, who were anything but slow. The sign decayed over the years, and now it's long since gone.

We went to the school plays, children stomping about on the dusty stage, saying their lines with the eccentric intonation the drama teacher taught them, bright choruses of the younger ones below the stage, old piano on the side. The last play was in 2014, as was the last school concert, the last sports day with the last picnic, hilariously trying to find the right event, keeping track of dogs and children.

Their childhood. I felt like it would last forever but I blinked and it was gone.

And for all the happy moments, that time was also shot through with anxiety and guilt, and enormous sadness for the children. They had had to witness, without understanding what they saw, the gradual disintegration and increasing reclusivity of their parents. They lost their home.

Hans and Eva loved their children; I know that. But isn't that also a cliché of parenting? What's the point of love if drugs come first?

People praised us for looking after them, but removing children from their parents is always an exercise of power. I don't think of it as an act of power over parents, though of course it is that, too. But primarily it's an act of power over children.

If Hans and Eva had been sober, they would never have portrayed themselves as the victims of this story. If they had been sober, they would have come down the day of the court case, bringing clothes and toys. If they had been sober they would have put up in a hotel nearby if they had to; they would have gone to the school to talk to the headmistress and teachers; they would have intervened in all ways possible to protect and help their children.

They didn't do any of that. But still my guilt gnawed at me, like a hum of nausea, merging with all my long-standing liberal suspicion of power.

. . .

I often thought about the discredited Cleveland and Orkney children's cases during those years. Those children had been removed from their homes by social workers, some in predawn raids. The children from the Scottish Orkney Islands were thought to have been abused in satanic rites. There was no evidence of that, beyond muddled answers to leading questions posed to children in the kind of repeated cross-examinations that even adults struggle to resist.

The children in Cleveland in the north of England were interrogated too, and subjected to the so-called reflex anal dilatation test, historically used to identify male homosexuals. Now the medical authorities allowed themselves the power of imitating the act of sodomising children to determine whether or not they had been sodomised. Was the purpose to help the children or to gather evidence against the parents? Who gave consent?

After much controversy, a report on the Cleveland case was commissioned, published in 1988. It found that the cases had been incorrectly handled. Ninety-four out of one hundred and twenty-one children were returned to their homes, and the dilatation test was discredited as a diagnostic tool for sexual abuse. The Orkney case ended in 1992, when an official inquiry report, strongly critical of the social workers, the police, and Orkney Islands Council, was published.

No wonder I thought about the Orkney and Cleveland children and their parents so much during and after our court case. I didn't regret what we had done, but the case was devastating for all of us. I take comfort from Adam Phillips' essay "Against Self-Criticism." "Guilt," he writes, "isn't necessarily a good clue as to what one values; it is only a good clue about what (or whom) one fears. Not doing something because one will feel guilty if one does it is not necessarily a good reason not to do it. Morality born of intimidation is immoral."

Looking back, I wish I could have been more robust in my own mind. The arguments in court were so outlandish that Eric never understood why I would even take them seriously: Hans and Eva were drug addicts, we took care of their children, and we were essentially accused of kidnapping them because we wanted more children? That made no sense.

To bring a case to court takes courage and single-mindedness. Eric, who had been banned and house-arrested as a young journalist reporting on human rights abuses and black politics in apartheid South Africa, and who had fled across the border to Botswana into fifteen years of exile in Britain, had any amount of courage and single-mindedness. I had a far more problematic and fraught perception of my own power. I also observed, more acutely, the pain and distress of the children.

That will always remain with us.

*

We now live mainly in London. I miss the country: the deer, the horses, the cattle, the scent mark of a fox drifting through the air, salt licks on muddy fields. I miss the white barn owl hunting low over the fields at dusk; the grey wagtail, every spring, tripping back and forth near the stream; the sea gulls sailing up on strong winds from the coast; the buzzards and the kestrels. I fed the horses every morning, and our pigeons, lined up on the dead branches of the old oak like strange white fruit. They would see me come and take off, swoop up and down, waiting for me to go. Mostly I did, but sometimes I stayed to watch them eat, studied them picking nervously at the seeds, an eye on me, an eye on the ground.

Even that felt to me like an illegitimate act of power. The pigeons were hungry; I forced fear on them.

Spring and early autumn evenings we played cricket and football. I fussed about the bats left on the lawn as the children ran inside, I lingered in the sudden silence, watching the sky and the rooks returning to the woods across the valley.

They are still there in the old house, the cricket bats, the tennis rackets, the baskets of balls and Frisbees and Hula-Hoops and dusty badminton sets.

It was a life.

8

In April 2008, nearly a year after the children came to live with us, Eva went to a party at the American embassy. She had some crack in her handbag, perhaps intentionally, perhaps not—it was found in a routine search on entry, and she was arrested. The police subsequently searched Hans and Eva's house and found small quantities of crack and heroin, and over three ounces of cocaine.

TETRA PAK HEIR HANS KRISTIAN RAUSING ADMITS POSSESSING COCAINE AND HEROIN ran one headline, and there were many others. Scotland Yard announced that Hans and Eva had been charged and bailed and were to appear in court later in the month.

Eva made a statement, stepping out of her front door in a short skirt and sunglasses and untidy blond hair, grinning conspiratorially at the photographers crowding the pavement below.

"I am very sorry for the upset I have caused," she said, reading from a piece of paper. "I intend to leave as soon as possible to seek the help that I very much need. I am ashamed of my actions; I hope in due course to get back on track to become the person I truly want to be."

I watch the footage and wonder again if this, in some sense, was just a game to her. It didn't seem quite real.

The refractions of addiction: authenticity and artificiality, pain and need and rebellion.

*

When I married my first husband, I converted to Judaism. We used to go to synagogue when Daniel was little, to lovely old West London Reform. Rabbi Winer would call the little children up to the bimah to drink a tiny silver thimbleful of wine. Most of the children would take a small sip and make a face, but Daniel, aged three or so, would down the little shot of wine and dance back to us with a beatific smile.

"Remember when I drank wine in synagogue?" he said, aged six. We already lived in the country then, far away from the synagogue.

"Yes! What did that feel like?" I asked.

"Like living in chocolateland," he answered, locking me with his eyes.

Sometimes on the way to school we would listen to Burl Ives singing "Big Rock Candy Mountain":

> *Oh . . . the buzzin' of the bees in the cigarette trees*
> *The soda water fountain*
> *where the lemonade springs*
> *And the bluebird sings*
> *in that Big Rock Candy Mountain.*

I love that bittersweet song, that mythical place,

Where a bum can stay for many a day
And he won't need any mo-o-ney

The cops have wooden legs, there, and the bulldogs have rubber teeth; there's a lake of gin for everyone, and the handouts grow on bushes.

Eva once told me about her dream of running a sweetshop in Knightsbridge—the never-never land of what might have been.

Instead she brought some crack to a party at the American embassy. What was she thinking? Maybe she'd forgotten it was there, a bag of drugs like dusty lozenges languishing in a handbag.

Hans and Eva were both charged with possession of a large amount of cocaine and smaller quantities of crack, heroin, and cannabis. But at Westminster Magistrates' Court, District Judge Timothy Workman determined that the proceedings would be formally discontinued. Hans and Eva received a conditional caution, along with some "rehabilitative or reparative conditions." Hans and Eva's solicitor said that there had been a "protracted course of correspondence from my office to the Crown Prosecution Service to enable them to make that very sensible decision."

The law is partly about what has actually happened and partly about intention. A lawyer could reasonably argue that wealthy clients, like Hans and Eva, had no intention to deal in drugs. They didn't need to. That is an argument which is harder to make for poor drug addicts, so bias creeps in: people who are poor (the majority of addicts) are much more likely to go to prison for drug offences, facing social stigma as well as the potential danger of overdosing after prison, following months of being relatively clean (drugs are smuggled into prisons, but it's hard to get daily heroin). When you are no longer habituated to heroin, what might have been a small dose months ago is now a deadly one.

We issued a statement. I wrote it.

> The Rausing family are deeply saddened by Hans Kristian's and Eva's situation, and the events leading up to their court appearance today.

> We hope with all our hearts that Hans Kristian and Eva can overcome their addiction and we continue to do what we can to help.

I wrote to Hans and Eva, too. "What will bring you back," I asked.

> There is no life without responsibility and agency.
>> There is only one life.
>> It's your choice.
>> Decisions.
>> Friendships.
>> Joy.
>> Please come back.
>> You are our family.
> Recovery is possible but you have to make that decision yourselves.

These letters are all the same. I have so many. I read them now, coldly bored by my own rhetoric, my stale ideas, the dull straws of recovery-speak.

Research has shown, incidentally, that it makes no difference whether or not people choose to go into care or are sentenced into care: the outcome is more or less the same. We thought the intention was the crucial thing. Turns out we were wrong: once someone is in a rehab they can be turned. Think of it as a process of deradicalisation. Because addiction is a culture of rebellion as much as it is an inherited disease or an emotional disorder.

*

We had all taken established dove or hawk positions by then. I was on the dove end of our spectrum; Peter, Lisbet's husband, and Eric were on the hawk end. Lisbet was more hawkish than me, but also more despairing. Our joint strategies were many and varied, and nothing helped.

One of the addiction experts we hired, an American working with wealthy families, tried to bond with my brother. He himself was an alcoholic in recovery. "I just showed Hans the family member handshake," he said to me at some anonymous hotel after another dismal strategy meeting.

"What's that?" I asked. He looked me straight in the eyes and started wagging his finger at me, laughing. Finger-wagging. Pointing, lecturing, admonishing. I got it: families are always tediously droning on: *responsibilities, friendships, joy, life, decisions, please come back, we are on your side.*

Our expert knew that landscape.

Tears stung my eyes.

Tears stung my eyes: a commonplace expression. But I know the meaning of it now. *Stinging tears* take you by surprise. They come quickly, before the conscious mind has fully registered the reason for crying.

They shame you, because you have no time to prepare.

*

I read up on Timothy Workman. He is an interesting judge. In 2003 he rightly refused to extradite the Chechen leader in exile Akhmed Zakayev to Russia. He also declined to extradite Russian oligarch and Putin-opponent, also in British exile, Boris Berezovsky, who later died in mysterious circumstances at his home in Berkshire. In 2005, Workman issued an arrest warrant for an Israeli army officer, Major General Doron Almog, after actions in Gaza. General Almog landed in London but stayed on the plane rather than risk arrest. Workman ordered extraditions to the United States of some Islamist terror suspects, refused bail to others, and in 2005 risked the ire of the British tabloids by apologising for scheduling a hearing on the day of Eid al-Fitr, the Muslim celebration of the end of Ramadan.

Timothy Workman was also a former probation officer, so he would have been familiar with the landscape of addiction. I assume he wanted to offer hope. I assume he had deduced that addicts don't do well in prison. But that conditional caution, those "rehabilitative or reparative conditions," came to nothing in the end.

*

In May 2009 I was concussed and lost some of my memory. I remember turning my horse for the gallop, leaning forward.

I remember the first part of the gallop, the horse's long mane whipping up into my face. I remember waking up on the grass, my broken helmet next to me. I lay there for some time before slowly getting up and walking home. I don't remember the fall. And after that, only fragments: a kind nurse sponging my teeth with cold water, another nurse combing my hair, and pulling it painfully. Liquid paracetamol in a drip. The pleasure of a thermal blanket filled with hot air when I was shaking with cold. Blue curtains around my bed. Eric coming and going, using all his persistence to get me an MRI on a Sunday in Kent and Sussex, the soon-to-be-closed hospital known locally as Kent and Snuff It.

I felt very calm. Swathes of memory were lost—I still don't know how much.

I search through my laptop, the thousands of messages and notes about meetings with lawyers, with addiction experts, with psychiatrists, with trustees. There are many abusive and deranged messages from Eva, and some from Hans, too. They were so angry.

I'd like to erase them all, but I don't. I have already lost too much memory, and it's an archive. I can't destroy it.

My son is nearly eighteen. I talk to him about drinking. "Don't drink," I say. "If you become an alcoholic I may have to shoot you." He laughs. I laugh, too, slightly bitterly, the metal aftertaste of bad history.

I try to explain about addiction as a family disease. The genetic component. I have to warn the children, but I mustn't let the theme of addiction become an obsession, a potentially self-fulfilling prophecy.

"Was Hans always an addict?" Daniel asks. "I mean, could you tell, even when he was a child?"

It's a good question. It's *the* question, of course. Mothers and fathers in every country in the world ask themselves the same thing, turning over childhood histories. Was it their fault? Did they cause this? Is addiction a reaction to immediate and recent events and people, the answer to contemporary needs and wants, or is it about childhood trauma? Is it one phenomenon for some people and something else entirely for others? Is it a response to pain? Is it an expression of a certain hollowing out, a process of incremental degeneration? Is it caused by a random encounter with habituating substances? Is it a second self, a predestined fate, or is it an accident; a cultural habit; a theatre of discontent, a seedy play of existential tragedy; a mode of being people take up one rainy day and can't, or won't, put down again?

There is such a thing as a *perfect storm*. The expression has two meanings: *a particularly violent storm arising from a rare combination of adverse meteorological factors* and *an especially bad situation caused by a combination of unfavourable circumstances*. Addiction is a perfect storm.

Hans and Eva. There they were, in that London townhouse. Those pristine rooms; that locked bedroom, dealers' numbers written on the wall.

That room was their world.

Towards the end of Strindberg's *A Dream Play*, Indra's daughter returns to the sphere of the gods. She now understands better what it means to be human:

> *So this is what it's like to be human . . .*
> *One misses even what one has not valued*

One regrets even what one has not broken . . .
One wants to walk away, one wants to stay . . .

I think about my regrets—there are so many. Like Strindberg's characters we were plagued by indecision and discord, forced onto a hamster wheel of interventions and regrets, interventions and regrets, interventions and regrets.

*

Meanwhile, the media interest carried on. There was always a line or two of casual background information in the newspapers.

> Tetra Pak was founded in Sweden in 1951 by Mr. Rausing's grandfather, Ruben Rausing, who invented a paper carton for storing milk. It became the world's biggest packing production company.

Where did that quote come from? I don't even know. The BBC site gave this information:

> Rausing dynasty
>   Founded in 1951 by Ruben Rausing in Lund, Sweden, Tetra Pak quickly grew into a global packing company.
>   Hans Rausing Senior was appointed managing director of the company in 1954. After decades at the helm, he sold his 50% share of the company to his brother Gad Rausing, who died in 2000.

At the bottom of the web page is a box, with "More England Stories":

SUICIDE MOTHER GAVE GIRLS ACID DRINK

JAIL FOR PC WHO STABBED WIFE 81 TIMES

HEN PARTY DEATH LORRY DRIVER CLEARED

"Men are to be pitied."

Or as Caryl Churchill's translation has it: "People are so fucked up."

9

After the initial court hearing in May 2007, when the children first came to live with us in the country, Hans and Eva occasionally came to see them. The visits, however, gradually dwindled. Hans's last visit was in the summer of 2008, on his birthday. He came alone.

I made a cake for him. I baked it in the oven and let it cool. I cut it into three layers. I whipped cream and spread each layer thickly: the Swedish way. I covered the top of the cake in raspberries and grated dark chocolate over it. It was a pretty cake—a modest and symbolic monument to love and to simplicity, in the face of Hans and Eva's rejection of the small, the cosy, the sincere. It was a gesture towards the maternal and the domestic; the practices I fumbled so blindly to reach. Not too much, I thought—not an excess of virtue, not a smug rebuke.

I stood in my apron, by the Aga. A picture of motherhood. But this was beyond mothering, of course. The cake was a symbol and a gift, but it was a reminder of origins, too. When I was a child we used to make cakes in the summer from cake mixtures—how delicious they were, those mixtures, that lost modernity. Pour the mix in a bowl, add water. Make cake, then lick the plastic bowl, feel the clingy aftertaste of bitter baking powder.

We ate lunch. We ate the cake. We sang. Hans blew out the candles.

He swam with the children. He jumped into the swimming pool with his glasses on. He lost the glasses and found them on the bottom of the pool.

Then he sat at the kitchen table with the children and they drifted away one by one until only the youngest was left. Hans was still speaking, but his eyes were closing; he couldn't stay awake. Sometime in between lunch and tea he had, I assumed, taken something—most probably a morphine tablet or methadone. I would have smelled the heroin if he had smoked it, and he never injected.

Suddenly he decided to leave. I went with him to his car; I tried to stop him from driving off, but I couldn't.

Afterwards I thought I didn't try enough. I could have blocked the drive if I had been faster and stronger, but I didn't. I held the car door; he wrenched it out of my hand.

"You can't drive. I will have to call the police," I said, shrill and desperate. Worse than dull, now.

He drove off, wheels screeching.

Eric called the police: I couldn't bring myself to do it.

This perennial sense that I could have stopped him. Always this sense that when I tried I didn't try hard enough, so that trying itself became damaging rather than reparative. "Help," not help. My good intentions.

I didn't see Hans again for six years.

*

Eva's last visit was a few months later—I think it was sometime in September 2008, a weekend, summer still lingering, but I am not sure. She arrived on a late-afternoon train, and I picked her up from the small station outside the village. A few people got off, Eva amongst them. Her legs were emaciated, her eyes glazed. The children drifted away from her, too, but I am not sure whether she really noticed. She sat with me in the living room and chatted, calmly, about this and that. After a while she decided to leave, and I drove her back to the station.

I never saw her again.

She didn't stop writing, though. Her texts and emails were relentless. She had started dabbling in Kabbalah, and her communications were punctuated with references to G-d and to evil. She commanded me to obey her; she commanded me to go to hell. She called herself *omniscient* and *omnipresent*, she referred to herself as *almighty, eternal, infinite; evermore, everpresent, everlasting Eva.*

All those texts in the middle of the night on my old Nokia phone, often ending with a standard message about [more data being received] or whatever phones said in those days in response to texts that were too long to download. Her emails were even longer, full of craziness, self-pity and anger. But I also find the sadness in them now, in between the abuse and the outlandish accusations, like silver thread in a tapestry.

"If something should happen to me do not leave him alone," she wrote about Hans on January 18 in 2011. "Section him"— have him certified—"if you have to but don't leave him alone at least for a couple of weeks. I'm not planning anything but I'm scared my heart is going to fail. I am too sad and I sometimes hope that G-d will take me away to wait elsewhere for my children and Hans. It is not at all because I didn't love them enough. On the contrary, I loved them so much my heart may explode.

I have died once before during an operation and I know what happens to us."

In between these glimpses of something real and human (I hesitate to write those words, because of course everything we do is real and human by definition, but take it as shorthand for something honest, or at least believable) she returned to the same themes over and over again: that she couldn't see the children because then they would think that she was dangerous since the court had ordered that she could see them only under supervision; that we had bribed the judge, the social workers and the psychiatrists; that people—her secretary, her accountant, her trustees, her staff—stole from her or physically attacked her; that she had special powers because she had "died" during her heart operation in 2006.

Looking through my records again I find an old text from Eva, a typical text. She told me I had driven a stake through her heart, and nails through her palms; that she was in unbearable pain. She said I had lied in court, and stolen her children. She told me that she would never forgive me: "I despise you with an intensity that is not describable," she wrote.

I try to understand why she wrote that particular text. It arrived late at night, and I check my inbox for that day, to see what was going on. I find an email from Lisbet about a meeting at the children's school. It was well meant, innocent and kind, and yet reading it I can see that it might have triggered Eva's rage. Lisbet had sent the email to Eva's parents as well as to us and to our nanny Mel, and they might have forwarded it to Eva. It must have been one of Lisbet's weekends—sometimes she and Peter looked after the children, at our house. Those were the weekends when Daniel went to stay with his father in London, and Eric and I would go to London, too. Sunday afternoons we would pick Daniel up, drive back to the country, and get ready for the week to come.

Sun 7th Sep 2008

Hi everyone,

I went to the Year 6 meeting at the school on Saturday, Daniel's year. Here is what they said:

There will be a bit of academic streaming but no proper scholarship stream, and kids typically move up and down. It is important the kids don't feel an elite is being selected.

Homework diaries are key: check and sign prep diaries every day. Don't do the children's homework (although make sure they do their homework). It is more important the teachers know if the kid can't do something. If you have concerns, note them in the prep diary. Every prep should only take half an hour: they can stop if they are not done then.

The children will be tired with the extra work and they need to rest a lot, and eat healthily, at home.

Mr. W is the Child Protection Officer and the school will report any more serious worries they have about children to the Children's Services, if at all possible talking to parents first, but not if it is an emergency.

This is the year—this autumn really—when senior schools must be selected. Remember lists fill up fast. Provisional places must be arranged.

There is a new expanded salad bar at lunch.

The kids will get work that is only due a week from now—and no advance warnings of exams. They need to learn to space and pace their work: to become self-motivated and self-organized.

They will all do the ESB, English Speaking Board: family are warmly welcome to come hear their child.

They will have a great camping trip in summer term.

Summer term is an excellent time to start full-time or weekly boarding. They whizz around and have fun in the summer weather. There will be a taster boarder weekend soon. There are lots of Friday night boarders in this year.

It is not decided if Year 6 will do a play this year.

There should have been a letter from the form teacher this weekend (I didn't find it but perhaps you, Mel, will?).

As ever,

Lisbet

Such a kind email, such careful attention to detail. But if your children have been removed by a court, an email like that might well make you despair. All those cosy details of extended salad bars and camping trips; the note about the English Speaking Board, the ritual when eleven-year-old children speak without notes on their chosen subject, families and friends willing them on; all that, and the slightly sinister reference to child protection issues, might feel like nails driven through palms.

I feel weighed down with guilt, making this possible connection. But I also know this: there is no addict story that doesn't revolve around guilt. We were all guilty, and we were none of us guilty. We were trying to deal with a tragedy bigger than ourselves; one that we were as ill equipped to handle as anyone else, despite all our lawyers and addiction experts. Eva may never have seen Lisbet's letter. She could have randomly sent her own despairing communication on the same date. But I am looking for logic, for cause and effect. I am trying to solve the riddles and elucidate the remaining questions.

We did genuinely and sincerely try to help, I know that. But it wasn't the help Hans and Eva wanted, or needed: "I am unable to see things the way that you do, consequently I do not feel 'helped,'" Eva wrote to me in January 2011. "I feel broken, damaged, very badly hurt and I sense that I am going to die soon."

I didn't believe her, but she was right.

*

On the twenty-ninth of May 2011 Eva wrote a long email to me, which ended on a sad note:

"I don't think that I am nearly as strong as maybe people thought. In the same way that nobody had any idea how deeply I loved my children as I kept it hidden."

"Thank you for reading all of this Sigrid. I talk to so few people. You have no idea."

"I am still your Eva X"

I responded by trying to get her to see the children:

They miss you very much and would like, obviously, to see you. It's not too late. I wish I could persuade you to

put your pride on one side, and your wounded feelings
and your humiliation, your anger and your resent-
ment. I wish I could persuade you to try and rebuild
the relationship with the children—to put them first,
not yourselves. Since you haven't done it I assume
there must be a part of you that feels they are better off
without you. But I don't believe that to be true. They
would, I think, very much like to see you, and would be
happy to see you—there is a wound in them of missing you that is not getting better. Even if they may not
think of you every day (though I believe they do), they
still miss you, and need you.

On the same night she wrote to me, Eva had also written
to our solicitor in the children's case, accusing her of fraudu-
lently changing our affidavits to the court in the case about
the children—a claim that came up repeatedly. Hans and Eva
couldn't remember—and couldn't keep track of—the affidavits,
and they often accused us of making claims that we had never
made. They lost the court papers; we sent copies that were dismissed as fake. We requested and sent certified court records;
those papers, too, were lost or dismissed.

My puppy is on the carpet sleeping, his nose pressed against one
of my discarded socks. His lead is next to him on the floor; the
window is rattling slightly in the wind.

I remember Sussex social services in this room—Eva had
written to them claiming that Eric was homosexual, and that I
was depressed and on drugs. We were not, therefore, suitable
carers for their children. The Brighton social workers who came
for a home visit were in an awkward situation: they had to inves-

tigate us, but they also felt compelled to communicate their disapproval of the implicit homophobia of Eva's letter.

The investigation itself didn't take long—a conversation,
followed by an observation of our interaction with the children
in the kitchen. We were being judged, of course, but it was done
with a light touch. Only two of the children were at home. My
niece pressed herself against our nanny Mel and smiled shyly.
My nephew pressed himself against me, giggling. Mel smiled
ironically, and even the dogs seemed to be amused by this theatre
of the absurd.

10

In May 2012, all communications ceased. There was radio silence. Virtually all our exchanges had been with Eva, not with Hans—she was an avid communicator, and when she stopped, there was silence.

There was a rumour that she had left with Hans on June 12. One of the cars was gone. There had been pillows in the car, someone said. What did that mean? We sucked on scanty facts, asking one another useless questions, questions we knew had no answers; questions we knew would lead to no action. We had dwelled for too long in the realm of *trying to find things out*, of *keeping an eye on*, of *reports*.

No good could come of that, we knew.

But . . . had she gone back to America?

Had anyone seen her passport?

How could we find out . . . ?

I think we had already let go, by then. The questions were rhetorical.

A kind of hiatus opened up.

*

In late May 2012 my mother was hospitalised to investigate some new and alarming symptoms—she had unusual stomach pains and felt anxious. I had organised the admission and was taking her to the hospital. She came to our house to have lunch beforehand. At the house she missed a step and fell heavily backwards, hitting her head on a wooden step. She was eighty-two years old, and I thought we would have to call an ambulance, but strangely she seemed hardly to notice. We went to the hospital as planned, and she was examined there. She wasn't concussed and never mentioned it again.

The doctors found nothing physically wrong with her.

Looking back on it, I think the sudden silence from Hans and Eva had caused a subterranean panic, making her ill with anxiety. She sensed, I think, what we didn't: the potential meaning of silence.

*

Sunday, July 8 we flew to Sweden, with the children, our dog Leo, and my sister. We were so happy in the plane, pointing out landmarks to one another. There was the sea! There was the village! There was the island! The children were talking and laughing. Leo was smiling broadly and wagging his tail, half closing his eyes in contentment.

It was lovely—almost too lovely. We landed and stood on the tarmac of the small rural airport, greeted by a kind policeman acting as immigration officer. We gathered passports; we watched the high blue sky.

There was suddenly an eerie feeling in the air; an ominous note.

"I feel like something is going to happen," I said to Eric.

. . .

On the following day, July 9, 2012, Hans was arrested on Wandsworth Bridge in London, and his terrible life unravelled.

I had a scheduled call at 2:30 p.m. that day about human rights in Belarus. And then, so quickly, so easily, Eric stepped into my office. He had written a note: *"They have found Eva's body."*

I looked at it, briefly, while my interlocutor continued talking about Andrei Sannikov, the presidential candidate who had been jailed by President Lukashenko.

I stared at Eric. I couldn't breathe. I couldn't move. Time stilled. Eric stood with his note, ready to act, looking at me, waiting for me.

Leo stretched on the floor, oblivious to the shocking present.

They have found Eva's body.

What is that underwater quality of shock? That sense of slow motion, that sudden weight of invisible and silencing substance?

As yet we knew nothing, beyond the fact that a body had been found, presumed to be Eva.

My atheist legacy, that sentence. I guess the formulation should be in the possessive form . . . *a body had been found, presumed to be Eva's.* You possess your body in death, even though you have lost it, or it has lost you. But in real life, as I sometimes say to the children, in real life . . . was the body Eva, or was the body *Eva's?*

I don't know.

What is life?

The infinite and infinitesimal part of Eva that was *her life* was gone.

A body had been found, presumed to be Eva's.

That must be right.

Eva was gone; they found her body.

But in fact all we knew was this: *a body had been found.*

Soon we knew more. It was worse than we thought. The body—by now referred to as *human remains*—had been found in the bedroom on the second floor. It had been there for a long time.

Within a day we knew that it was Eva. She had died, probably, of a heart attack, but all we knew was that she was dead.

This is what we heard: that Hans had piled clothes on top of her and wrapped the body in a tarpaulin. He had stuck duct tape around the door to what the press later referred to as the "annexe" of their house—the bedroom, dressing room, and bathroom. It was, the papers said, a drug den.

Drug den is just an expression of course. Clothes all over the floor. Bottles, trash.

The body wrapped in a tarpaulin and hidden under the top mattress, under a flat-screen TV.

*

Hans, at this stage, was taking enough morphine every day to kill a small horse, I was told. He had been on the floor of a police cell, in agony, offered a paracetamol for withdrawal. He was catatonic with withdrawal, shock and grief, and was soon moved to hospital for medically supervised detoxification.

Enough morphine to kill a small horse. It seemed an odd analogy to me, since animals react so differently to drugs. I didn't understand what it meant—was that enough daily morphine to kill several people? I was confused by the analogy, my mind leaping to all the horses I have known; my grandfather and his racehorses, our stables, our past.

I genuinely wanted to know how horses react to morphine.

Try to think of something else. How many times have I heard my mother say that. Try to think of something else.

*

Revealing death. Telling the story.
   Telling children that their mother has died.
   They were so young.

Within hours the story had broken on the news. A stream of emails, with subject lines such as *thinking of you, sending love, condolences, Eva,* started coming in. Soon there were letters, too.
   There was an avalanche of media, journalists and photographers everywhere. We saw the vans from the house; the photographers with their cameras.
   For a brief moment Hans was suspected of murder. I

remember saying to the children that this did not mean that he was guilty, or that anyone thought he was. They looked at me with blank eyes.

As the world now knows, Eva Rausing's dead body was discovered at her £70 million Chelsea mansion last Monday. She was 48 years old.

Her husband, Hans Kristian, joint heir to the £4.5 billion Tetra Pak packaging fortune has been arrested on suspicion of murder.

Daily Mail, July 14, 2012

*

Soon the children left, my son to visit his father, the others to America, to Eva's sister and parents.

The hares were boxing; the herring gulls were crying.

Swirling clouds of starlings gathered at dusk, flying towards the marsh beyond the harbour. We watched the sunset evening after evening.

Eric and I stayed in Sweden to be near my parents. They were in the house next door, in the old cottage.

Eric cooked for me. We played chess over lunch and dinner at the kitchen table, as we do. I lost time after time. I lost twenty-three games in a row.

We didn't watch the news or read the papers.

What did we do? I don't remember. We sat with my parents.

We watched *The Battle of Algiers* again, Gillo Pontecorvo's epic 1960s film about the Algerian struggle for independence, terrorist bombs, and French repression and torture.

Every few hours I cried until I couldn't breathe. In between the waves of grief I was exhausted, still.

Time distorted.

Leo followed me from room to room in the quiet house.

The eye of the storm. It was so peaceful there.

II

Eva died on May 7, 2012. The inquest took place in December of that year. Hans testified that he'd been there when she died. He had said to his psychiatrist that she looked peaceful. Also childlike.

She had come back from a rehab in California a few days before she died. Later we heard that she had been asked to leave for bringing in drugs. That may not be true.

The media published endless last pictures of her, claiming that she looked "gaunt" and "unwell." I look at the photographs and think, to the contrary, how well she looked, compared with when I last saw her, in 2008. She had filled out, and her hair was long. Her legs were a little swollen, perhaps, but not obviously so.

I find the last recording of Eva online, incidental footage someone had taken on the street.

It's true that she is not quite steady on her feet. Hans had driven her, apparently, to the dentist. He—also not quite steady, and quite grey and stooped—gets out of the car and helps her out. She asks him a question. He points in response, possibly to show her the entrance to the dentist's office.

. . .

I watch the clip again and again. I hadn't seen either of them for four years.

*

When we were small, on long journeys or on walks, my father used to play a game with us: what would we do if humanity had died out, and we were alone in a post-apocalyptic world? How would we live, and where? Survival was the object, and there were dangers everywhere: starvation, infections, feral dogs. My father suggested scenarios with reference to ancient history and traditional methods of food preservation; to dogs hunting in packs; to wild sources of protein and vitamins. We tried to think of solutions, which suggested consequences, and other problems.

My mind still sometimes wanders to that game, to fantasies of aloneness: scavenging in abandoned farmhouses and super-markets, releasing horses trapped in stables, sailing across the channel, going south.

I think of Hans and Eva in their locked room, their decaying teeth.

Drugs dull the capacity to feel. And without emotions we can't live. I read in the *New Scientist* or *Scientific American* that fruit flies get "unsettled" by shadows mimicking predator wings. Fear, of course, is critical to survival: flies with fear would have a tremendous evolutionary edge over flies without fear. Animals need emotions to survive. And so do we.

Without emotions you can become a castaway in the heart of London. A scavenger in your own house.

*

May 7, early morning. The early hour was, I assume, in fact a late hour of the night before—Hans and Eva lived nocturnal lives, and she must have been jet-lagged from California, from that week in the rehab. May 6, then.
A Sunday. Then a Monday.

*

After his arrest on Wandsworth Bridge, Hans ended up in hospital for detox and drug treatment.

The court hearing was on August 1. Hans spoke only twice, to confirm his name and to plead guilty to the charge of preventing the decent and lawful burial of his wife. He was essentially sentenced into care: a short suspended prison sentence and a two-year drug rehabilitation program.

He had made a statement to the police which was read to the court. He was devastated and traumatised by Eva's death, he said. He did not have a coherent recollection of the events leading up to her death. He had never wished her any harm, nor had he ever done her any harm, or supplied her with drugs.

"I did not feel able to confront the reality of her death . . . I tried to carry on as if her death had not happened. I batted away inquiries about her. I took some measures to reduce the smell."

"I believe in the period since she died I have suffered some form of breakdown."

*

I talk to my psychoanalyst about my brother's ability to *carry on* as if Eva's death had not happened. He interprets it as an extreme form of splitting. I hear him on the telephone, getting up and walking to the bookcase, getting a book out. He is looking for a particular case study, he says, by the analyst Herbert Rosenfeld, about a patient, Caroline, who was also in analytic training.

Herbert Rosenfeld was born in Germany in 1910, and left for Britain, a Jewish refugee, in 1935. He was already a doctor, but had to retake his medical degree in Britain, and eventually specialised in psychoanalysis, trained by Melanie Klein. There is a photograph of him on the Melanie Klein Trust site: he sits, an old man, in a crumpled white V-necked sweater, a slightly wry smile. Why is this picture so compelling to me? Is it the sense that he could have made it right, this sorry story; that he could have rescued Hans and Eva and said wise and memorable things to all of us?

Rosenfeld's 1987 book, *Impasse and Interpretation*, is about the problem of impasse in the psychoanalytic process, when the conversation between patient and analyst, and the interest, the spark, transference and countertransference, wane. This waning is really the subject of the whole book, and there are many other case studies in it, some of them as dramatic as the case of Caroline. Rosenfeld's thesis is that these impasses can, if properly analysed, reveal something interesting about the patient's psyche. Conversely, if the impasse is not dealt with carefully it can become dangerous, and detrimental to the patient's mental health. The analyst must pay attention to an impasse, therefore, and handle it with care.

Caroline was in analytic training, both a patient and a student. She seemed happy and stable, though she was perhaps, he writes, "slightly manic," and arrived with a self-diagnosis of "schizoid personality." There were really only two incidents that worried him: Caroline thought that the nurses in the clinic where she worked spied on her, suspecting her of drug taking, and she was dismissed from her work in the clinic, because, she said, of some "misunderstanding" or "misrepresentation."

Caroline's ambition, in which she eventually succeeded, was to become director of a clinic for drug addicts. But her assistant there reported her to the police: she had, he claimed, sold drug prescriptions to addicts for large sums of money. Her solicitor investigated and found the charge to be true. He approached Rosenfeld, asking him to support a defence of schizophrenia in court. Caroline, meanwhile, claimed to be both sane and innocent in letters from detention—a tricky defence in the face of the overwhelming evidence. "This put me in a difficult position," Rosenfeld writes, with beguiling frankness.

Then, astonishingly, Caroline tried to hire a hitman from prison to kill the assistant who had reported her to the police. She was placed under psychiatric observation at a mental hospital, where she was found to be sane. After being found guilty in the subsequent court case, however, feelings of acute persecution and disturbance developed. Schizophrenia was eventually diagnosed after all, and Caroline was detained, potentially indefinitely, in a mental hospital.

Rosenfeld came to believe, he wrote, that Caroline had a "destructive, murderous, and criminal part of her personality which was both so completely split off, and, eventually, so powerful and so serious that I came to know about it (along with her husband, and, indeed, in some ways Caroline herself) only through a newspaper story and the intervention of the police."

. . .

If Caroline was a drug addict, Rosenfeld doesn't say so, but whether or not she was, drugs play a part in this story. His ambivalence about the degree of Caroline's moral culpability is of course inherent in psychoanalysis, but it also reflects our confusion about innocence or guilt in the context of drugs. We haven't agreed, as a society, how far drug addicts are guilty of their many and varied trespasses against the law, their families, and social norms. You can't be found both insane and guilty— you are one or the other. Insanity rules out culpability; culpability rules out insanity. But addicts have a foot in each camp, and in that confusion, that fog of mental shrugs, that bleak no man's land between our perception of individual self-determination and the mental illness of cravings and compulsion, people die, children are neglected, and families split apart.

I am not suggesting that defining the border between innocence and guilt, or compulsion and free will, is easy, either philosophically or legally. I support the principles of human rights, and I am aware of the dubious history of many psychiatric diagnoses and treatments, some of them forced. Homosexuality was regarded as a serious mental disorder in the United States until 1973. More recently, the discredited school of therapy which was based on excavating "recovered memories" of sexual abuse from patients (mainly women), who exhibited symptoms which had come to be strongly associated with sexual abuse, led to the prosecution of more than a hundred alleged abusers (mainly men), most or all of whom were probably innocent.

Note the "most or all." I wrote it automatically, in case some of them in fact were guilty. This is why the stigma will be with them for life. No one will ever know whether their innocence has been, or can be, established beyond doubt. All one can know is that the methodology of recovered memory therapy has been discredited. But haven't we all learnt, don't we all believe, that the absence of evidence is not the same as the evidence of absence?

I was a member of an NSPCC (National Society for the Prevention of Cruelty to Children) fundraising board when the Cleveland case happened. When I expressed concern about the case to a staff member—the dawn raids, the intrusive and uncertain tests—he said that *there was no smoke without fire.*

No smoke without fire. No matter that according to law people are innocent until proven guilty. No matter that whether the parents were guilty or not the state also abused the children by subjecting them to dawn raids and the dilatation test.

Recovered memory therapy ended (or should have ended) in the early 1990s, when professor Elizabeth Loftus at the University of Washington devised a series of psychological experiments which showed how easy it is to implant false memories by suggestion. But the idea of repressed memories lingers on.

Perhaps there can be no true criminal guilt in the psychoanalytic context. Most references to guilt in the psychoanalytic literature are about neurotic preoccupations with forgotten (or repressed) childhood observations or transgressions. People who feel that kind of guilt are innocent by definition. What makes Rosenfeld's case study of Caroline so interesting is that she really was guilty, and he didn't quite know what to make of that guilt. He had to decide whether or not to support a schizophrenia defence, but he was also facing the broader question of how you diagnose and treat someone who seems sane, and who claims to be innocent, while acting so criminally.

This case has all the ingredients of addiction: drugs, denial, paranoia, greed, and criminality. Addiction is nearly always situated in that borderland between criminality and disease; between sincerity and insincerity; between honesty and lies; between pleasure and pain.

Rosenfeld's implication is that Caroline herself was partially unaware of her actions: he trusted her story. But how can you trust anyone's story? Every story, including mine, is an enactment of what we wish to be true, an edited version of our selves.

I think of Madame Bovary's feverish talks with her lover, Léon, about death, about illness and suffering, about how they both long for "the quiet of the grave." Emma and Léon, Flaubert wrote, devised for each other ". . . an ideal rearrangement of their past. Language is indeed a machine that continually amplifies the emotions."

Language is indeed a machine that continually amplifies the emotions.

Psychoanalytic theory postulates that sons harbour a concealed wish to kill (actually or symbolically) their fathers. In popular culture, this is turned on its head: successful fathers are said to doom their sons to failure. "In the shadow of greatness God takes a rest," the cruel joke goes. It's a harsh concept, either way.

Fathers and sons. Think of Hamlet, perpetually in psychic motion, leaning towards acting, double meanings and mixed messages. The play is about generational clashes, surveillance of the young, uncertainty of culpability, loss of mind, suicide. We know those issues. They are as current now as they were then.

Freud, conflating text and life, analysed Hamlet's ambivalence as a concealed identification with his father's murderer. His own repressed desire to kill his father has been realised:

Thus the loathing which should drive him on to revenge is replaced in him by self-reproaches, by scruples of conscience, which remind him that he himself is literally no better than the sinner whom he is to punish.

The French psychoanalyst Nicolas Abraham wrote a sequel to Shakespeare's play, *The Phantom of Hamlet or The Sixth Act*, about the riddle of the ghost—he saw a complex hidden political drama in the play, which Hamlet, unconsciously motivated by filial duty and respect, refused to see.

But what if Shakespeare didn't intend us to believe in the device of the ghost? What if Hamlet's uncle and mother did not conspire to kill his father? Assume their innocence, read the play, and watch Hamlet wreak havoc with his delusions.

Or take Thomas Vinterberg's film, *Festen*, about wealth, power, and sexual abuse. Someone told the story on an emotional call-in radio show, and Vinterberg assumed that it was true. But it turned out it wasn't true. The caller had created a fictional narrative. In real life, his father was innocent. The father protagonist in the film—conservative, racist, abusive— was a figment of the imagination. We know the type. But watch *Festen* knowing the father to be innocent, tweak the script, and see a troubled son destroying a family.

Most people believe that mental pain must have a cause which is proportional to the pain. But that may not be so—our psyches are not necessarily so finely balanced in terms of cause and effect. And yet behind any story of compulsion and addiction, there is still a hinterland of suffering. For one thing, to act in secret, as almost all addicts do, is to fear exposure and some form of intervention. But the secrecy and fear of consequences is only part of it. You can trust the fact of suffering, even if you can't necessarily trust the particular narrative crystallising around the suffering. Only the subtext is reliable, that which is not stated, the distress which is so obvious even as it is denied by the addicts and sometimes also denied by those around them who are blinded by their own powerful psychological mechanisms, their own leanings towards enabling and collusion.

That tendency to look the other way when it comes to addiction, the tendency to call it and then not call it, to diagnose it and then undiagnose it, is so pervasive. Addiction is a sensitive subject. Even *DSM-5*, the American diagnostic handbook of mental disorders, ties itself up in knots about language:

> Note that the word *addiction* is not applied as a diagnostic term in this classification, although it is in common usage in many countries to describe severe problems related to compulsive and habitual use of substances. The more neutral *substance use disorder* is used to describe the wide range of the disorder, from a mild form to a severe state of chronically relapsing, compulsive drug taking. Some clinicians will choose to use the word *addiction* to describe more extreme presentations, but the word is omitted from the official *DSM-5* substance use disorder diagnostic terminology because of its uncertain definition and its potentially negative connotation.

Potentially negative connotation. I feel a wave of bitter irony.

*

Joan Didion's novel *Play It as It Lays* describes the breakdown of a Hollywood actress, Maria Wyeth, in the early 1960s. Maria takes to compulsively driving up and down the freeways: "She drove the San Diego to the Harbor, the Harbor up to the Holly-wood, the Hollywood to the Golden State, the Santa Monica, the Santa Ana, the Pasadena, the Ventura."

She would stand on the hot pavement and drink the Coke from the bottle and put the bottle back in the rack (she tried always to let the attendant notice her putting the bottle in the rack, a show of thoughtful responsibil-ity, no sardine cans in her sink) and then she would walk to the edge of the concrete and stand, letting the sun dry her damp back.

Maria Wyeth is enacting a story where she is not alone, where there are no empty sardine cans in the sink, where she hasn't broken down. She sleeps outside on an old rattan chaise by the pool, using beach towels for blankets to mark the tempo-rary nature of the chaise as bed; to break the slide towards those empty cans and bottles, the point of no return. She tells herself a story about sleeping outside only until the heat breaks; until the mountain fires stop; because she is bothered by the palm fronds scraping the screens of her windows.

We tell ourselves such stories every day. We tell the story of ourselves to others. If no one listens we tell the story of our-selves into the void, or the Internet. But addicts, more than most people (and we are all somewhere on the spectrum of addiction), create stories of blame and denial: they deny that drugs are a problem, and they tend to blame others for any problems that may be undeniable in their lives. But here is a paradox: the spo-ken narrative is based on denial, while the enactment—addict life—is visually, and obviously, horrific.

Addicts live in a drug bubble. They are numbed by drugs

and, unlike Didion's Maria Wyeth, they don't notice much; neglect creeps in. But I still wonder about that contradiction: are addicts unconsciously trying to draw attention to an emotional state that they are unable to express in words? Is addiction associated with a certain inarticulacy, so that instead of narrating a disturbed emotional state—*I feel so awful, I am so sad, I feel hopeless*—they mutely enact it, even as they deny it?

Maria Wyeth tried to act normal. What if addicts unconsciously enact a profound emotional need or disturbance while simultaneously denying it; dark and truthful ids hijacked by bright and shallow superegos?

Eva in front of the mirror, dusting the skin over her pacemaker below her collarbone with powder, making light of it. That flat square, inserted under the living skin, keeping the heart beating.

Ids hijacked by superegos. I keep coming back to the idea of the kidnap, the hostage, the prisoner. Addiction is a family disease, they say. An endlessly revolving merry-go-round of guards and hostages, addicts and family members alternating roles.

*

Remember the painting at Tate Britain, *The Worship of Bacchus*, by George Cruikshank? "Sacrificed at the shrine of Bacchus, father, mother, sister, brother, wife, children, property, friends, body and mind."

Have we lost sight of the fact that somewhere in that sacrifice there is volition, or at least *akrasia*, the deficiency of will described by Walter Mischel? Recovering addicts know that before you reach the point of no return there are many turns in the road. The strength of the 12-step programs is that they combine an emphasis on that moral journey with a principled lack of moralising, or judgemental blaming. The disease model bypasses the question of blame and guilt, ignoring the whole thorny issue of causation, which so often leads addicts to speculation and self-pity, to blame and denial. True recovery is a profoundly ethical journey, finding meaning and dignity through solidarity and restitution. Without that, there may be a cessation of drinking or substance use, but there is no real recovery.

I sound so moralistic, so prim—so proud of the neat fences, the geraniums on the windowsill.

The finger wags and wags.

But I don't know how else to talk about it.

How do you write about addiction? How do you disentangle it from rebellion, or from social protest? The drug user is marking her body, she's leaving home. It's an adventure; then she steals and lies—she has to, to get by. Marks on the body, marks on the soul. She is not an addict yet; or maybe she is. How many people who use drugs turn into addicts?

We are snared in language and in traditions; the history of protest, the history of drugs. The 1970s runaways on the streets of San Francisco thought they were free, but then hard drugs hit them, and sexual abuse and HIV hit them. Some ended up with grey teeth and scarred arms in seedy rooms in the Ambassador Hotel: everything their parents, those imaginary hectoring and oppressive figures, grimly predicted.

They were not free, those runaways, were they?

Or maybe they were, for a while.

*

Eva's grandmother lived on the Upper East Side of Manhattan. I always used to imagine Eva there, too, in her Chanel suits and high heels, bedraggled but glamorous, a hint of chronic anorexia and too many prescription pills, shopping on Madison Avenue, white wine at lunch, gossip and occasional cheques for select good causes.

It could have been.

I lie on my window seat watching the trees, watching the Heathrow planes cross the sky punctuating time, one after the other, one after the other.

Why couldn't it have been?

There was a song in my head that awful year: "The Carnival Is Over." Not a song I really knew, but I found myself humming it, over and over. Such is the stuff our ids are made of—that is both thrilling and disappointing, in equal measure.

Two years later, I finally looked it up—the Seekers released it in 1965. They are mannered and slightly ironic in this 1967 recording; they are standing on a space age stage, before boarding a silver airplane. Their voices are steady and clear.

It's so kitschy. And yet I cry hearing it.

> *Say goodbye, my own true lover*
> *As we sing a lover's song*
> *How it breaks my heart to leave you*
> *Now the carnival is gone*
>
> *High above, the dawn is waking*
> *And my tears are falling rain*

For the carnival is over
We may never meet again

But the carnival is not really over. The carnival can always start again—the caged animals, the helter-skelter, the spun sugar and the music, the screams and the lights and the dark, the innocence and the guilt, the genetic thread running through us, weaving in and out of generations.

I watch myself. I watch my son. I watch my nieces and nephews. I watch for signs. They know this.

And perhaps the process of observation skews that which is being observed. I am watching for signs of addiction, but I also know that most people in distress will enact their diagnosis. A few people with psychiatric diagnoses become catatonic, but most of us, distressed or not, are more malleable.

Would we be better off if we assumed that this will never happen again? Are we creating a family model of addiction; an expectation of dysfunction?

These endless questions. The fate of families of the distressed is to always wonder what you have done, and what you haven't done.

In the autumn of 2012 I wrote to Hans in hospital, describing a dream I'd had. I hadn't seen him yet—he wasn't ready to see any of us. I dreamt that he was in a hotel, doing rehab. I saw him there. It was, as in real life, the first time I had seen him since 2008. His room was a suite, not big; the term "junior suite" was in my mind. At the back of the small living room was a black leather sofa, and sprawled on that sofa was a woman I knew to be his psychiatrist, a dream character lying with her back to me, bare stockinged feet up. Her high-heel shoes were on the carpet. Someone else—a lawyer or adviser—was in the room, too.

There was a certain disorder in the room, a frightening lack of boundaries. Hans welcomed me, but not warmly. Then he made chocolate milk with chocolate powder. It was messy.

The dream ended with a plane laboriously taking off. There were too many people on board, including a little girl who seemed to have no parents.

All the people we were meant to trust I didn't trust—the psychiatrist with her high heels, on the sofa, the adviser in the room. The chocolate powder and the child; the heroin and the addict. I had lost faith in our advisers, and like children with attachment disorders I kept my own counsel.

*

Six months later, I take my youngest nephew, then twelve, for lunch with my parents.

He is reluctant to come but finally does, with the promise that he can drive up our drive and down my parents' longer drive. "Anyone who can drive a go-cart can basically drive," I say before we set off, to encourage him. He has never driven before, but he can do it, easily. He brought his slingshot, also, to show my father.

My nephew is interested in science, and at lunch we talk about the beginning of the universe, the Big Bang, Einstein, and Schrödinger's cat. My father hears nothing my nephew says, and I repeat everything in my loudest, clearest voice. My father's lips are bloody from a treatment of precancerous cells; he is frail.

After lunch we go out to watch my nephew shoot his slingshot. "Shoot the girl!" my father says whimsically, pointing to a naked bronze statue whose hand trails the water of a fountain. My nephew shoots, and misses. "He wants to protect the girl, unconsciously," I say, filling a silence as I do. My father leans on my arm, so tall and not quite steady, nearly ninety. I feel such affection for him, such a sense of longing, even though he is right there, his large dry hand on my arm.

*

The months after Eva died I went over the sequence of events in my mind, over and over again. I wanted to know exactly what had happened. In the beginning we had few facts, but all our assumptions turned out to be true. It was such a simple story:

Eva had died of heart failure, as she herself had predicted many times that she would.

The inquest, which took place in December 2012, told us more. We learnt that Eva had been identified by the fingerprint on her left thumb and the serial number of her pacemaker. This was set at 65 beats per minute. On December 1, 2011, it recorded 334 beats per minute over a five-second period. On January 4, 2012, it recorded four episodes of a heartbeat between 233 and 366 beats per minute. On May 7 there were nine episodes of between 180 and 384 beats per minute.

I take my own pulse. Sixty-six beats per minute. I divide 334, the heartbeat of the five-second December 2011 episode, with 60, and multiply it with 5, and get 27.83. I try to drum twenty-seven times on my arm over five seconds, but I can't. I mumble a count, to see if I can count twenty-seven times over five seconds, but it's not possible. I get to eighteen or nineteen at most, counting as fast as I can. How can a heart beat so fast?

Each episode, presumably, is an inhalation of crack or cocaine.

At 7:23 a.m. on May 7 the rhythm of Eva's heart became chaotic. This was likely to have been the time of her death.

The pacemaker carried on, as pacemakers do.

*

She was found two months later, on Monday, July 9, 2012, after a policeman had stopped Hans for driving erratically across Wandsworth Bridge. There was a crack pipe in the car (a warm crack pipe, we heard) and a bag of letters addressed to Eva. There was heroin and cannabis in the car, too. When the police asked Hans if he knew where Eva was, he initially said, eyes welling up, that she was in California.

The officer, who was giving evidence at the inquest, said that Hans appeared "dishevelled" and "vacant." He suspected that drugs were involved, but he was also concerned about the letters addressed to Eva in the car and, potentially, a missing person case. The police initiated a Section 18 search of the house.

Section 18 is the part of the Police and Criminal Evidence Act of 1984 that covers police entry and search after arrest. An officer authorising (or being informed of) a search must make a written record of two things: the grounds for the search and the nature of the evidence that is sought. A suspicion of drugs, in this instance and no doubt in many others, gives the police an easy legal reason to search premises.

So the police turned up at Hans and Eva's house on that July day. They were taken to the first floor by staff. They noted that the house was immaculate and asked where Mr. Rausing slept. The housekeeper made a phone call before replying; it was clear that the housekeepers were not allowed in the bedroom. The officers went up to the second floor in the lift.

They noticed a smell of decomposition.

They walked into the bedroom. The policeman described it as looking like a "squat," "in a state of disarray." The bed was covered by a blue tarpaulin and several television screens. They saw a second door with duct tape around it and became concerned that someone might be held prisoner. They removed furniture and pulled the tape off, but found nothing sinister in the room next door.

They cleared away the televisions and some drawers on the bed and removed the tarpaulin. Underneath were blankets, duvets, and clothing, all covered in a white powder, perhaps some sort of deodorising powder. After many layers had been removed, they saw blond hair.

*

Hans's lawyers wrote a statement for the inquest. It seemed to have been written with the intention of minimising Hans and Eva's drug addiction, as though that would make Eva's death, and Hans's act of hiding Eva's body—the crime he was accused of—less serious. But of course Eva's death, and the act of hiding her body, are only comprehensible in terms of the profound dysfunction of addiction. Hans could only have done what he did because of the very serious nature of his addiction.

The statement outlined Hans's early addiction in one sentence. He was said to have attended rehab and "overcome" his illness. He and Eva married in 1992, had four children, and enjoyed a close relationship. On New Year's Eve 1999 Eva drank champagne, and Hans also (subsequently) began to drink. They were drinking and smoking marijuana but "remained in control." In 2007 there was a successful (and unexplained, in the statement) application for the children to be made wards of court.

From that time on, the lawyers wrote, Hans and Eva took increasing amounts of drugs, including morphine legitimately prescribed by doctors.

In August 2006 Eva Rausing had surgery to replace a valve in her heart, the statement continued. During surgery the heart was damaged, and a pacemaker had to be fitted.

In April 2012, she travelled to a rehabilitation clinic in Malibu. Then she returned home unexpectedly: it appeared that she had been asked to leave the clinic when she was found with Valium. Mr. Rausing was upset that the rehabilitation had not been successful.

The statement moved on to the events on May 7. Hans was shaving when he heard Eva slide off the bed. He saw her sitting on the floor beside the bed. She exhaled and went still. He tried to pull her up and shouted her name. She had stopped breathing, and he knew that she was dead.

He covered her up, the statement said, because he did not want to confront Eva's death. He tried to carry on as though it had not happened; he couldn't bear to tell her parents or the children.

At the time of the statement, he did not know the date of her death or how long she had been there.

*

Dr. Nathaniel Carey was the pathologist undertaking the post-mortem examination of the body. At the inquest, he noted that the pacemaker was helpful in determining the time of death, though he expressed reservations about whether the time on the pacemaker was British Summer Time or GMT (Greenwich Mean Time). The coroner in charge said that it would be sufficient to establish a date of death. Dr. Carey confirmed that after the burst of nonsurvivable heartbeat, the rhythm of the pacemaker was consistent with the heart no longer functioning.

Dr. Carey, I discover, is one of the most respected senior pathologists in the U.K. He was involved in the case of the two murdered schoolgirls in Soham, the Ipswich serial killings of prostitutes, and the death of former Russian agent Alexander Litvinenko, who was poisoned with polonium in London.

The coroner asked Dr. Carey about the postmortem examination. He reported that the body had been severely decomposed, limiting the scope for assessment, but that there were no obvious injuries or indications of natural disease. It was apparent that the deceased had had heart surgery. The tricuspid valve had been replaced and was functioning normally. He noted that disease of the right side of the heart commonly relates to intravenous drug abuse. A full assessment of the heart was not possible, he said, but the scarring of the heart muscles was consistent with long-term cocaine use. Dr. Carey also said that it is common for accident and emergency departments to see patients complaining of chest pains and abnormal rhythms as a result of drug abuse.

The toxicological examination of the calf muscle and liver showed that Eva had been intoxicated by cocaine at the time of death, and Dr. Carey felt it was safe to presume that it was cocaine intoxication which caused her heart disturbance. He confirmed that a pacemaker cannot prevent rhythm changes in the heart, unlike an implantable defibrillator.

On the balance of probabilities he concluded that the principal cause of death was cocaine intoxication, causing fatal arrhythmia in an already diseased and susceptible heart.

The coroner found that Dr. Carey had been able to rule out a violent death and establish that the death was not suspicious. Hans was therefore charged solely with preventing Eva's lawful burial. She concluded, on the balance of probabilities, that Eva had died on May 7, 2012. In the body there was clear evidence of cocaine use, and silver foil and wire wool found in the hands of the deceased also indicated recent inhalation of cocaine.

The coroner found that Eva had died as a result of cocaine

intoxication. Her tricuspid valve disease and its prior replacement were contributory factors.

Finally, she offered her condolences to the family for the loss of a forty-eight-year-old mother, wife, daughter, and sister.

*

One of the purposes of official reports is to make us feel safe again. Authority is restored. The coroner takes the evidence, sifts the facts, and writes conclusions based on medical and legal experience. The inquest represented reason and sanity, and when you have lived with dysfunction and addiction for so long, reason and sanity fill you with hope, like a tribunal or truth commission after political repression. The legal process imposes order on shifting sands—the facts may be shocking, but the steady legal narratives contain the facts and make them safe. Perhaps this was the account I was looking for, the text that could be filed in the family archive.

But in the end the authority of the inquest was not enough. My thirst for knowledge was too intense, and the story was inevitably simplified. The riddle wasn't solved. For instance, the coroner didn't say so, but the silver foil and wire wool in Eva's hands indicate crack cocaine, not powder cocaine.

Crack is cocaine mixed with water and baking soda, forming pink or brown rocks that can be smoked. I learn from the Internet that you can place the rocks on the foil and set them on fire and inhale, or you can use a glass pipe, inserting wire wool as a filter. The hit is faster and more intense than the hit of powder cocaine. The high is accompanied by a greatly increased heart rate and a risk of death from heart attack or stroke. It is followed by depression and edginess. Paranoia, anger, hostility, and anxiety are common and lasting side effects, along with severe tooth decay; damage to blood vessels, liver, kidneys, and lungs; malnutrition; confusion and psychosis.

*

The inside of a body.
    A body turned inside out.
    A fingerprint.
    A pacemaker, still beating its regular rhythm.
    A life, gone.

13

In February 2016, *Channel 4 News* broadcast a special report from Mombasa. The city is overrun with heroin, the reporter said; it has become the centre of a smuggling route from Afghanistan and Pakistan. The report comes with a warning: there are graphic images of drug taking and the use of needles.

These days there are always warnings on the news. We see painful images of war and terrorism, and even so, the reporters often say, they have images they can't show us; images that convey human suffering on a scale that we couldn't bear. This report is not about war, and yet it shows a world fragmented— a culture addicted. Tourists have abandoned Mombasa for fear of terrorism, and three out of four young people are unemployed. Addiction is the "new normal," the reporter says. He talks about weak maritime border controls and corruption, about drugs destined for Europe transiting through Mombasa. Some of the heroin is left behind, causing "misery for a generation." The city is said to be "littered with heroin addicts."

The film team go to a drug den: that word again. What is this place? A room, a shack? Addicts sit on a cement floor. There is a man they call the "doctor"; he is missing some teeth. His eyes are slow. The men inject their legs and hands. The camera

focuses on the entry point of the needle; the images are deliberately blurred; a grey digital balloon hovers over the skin. A man
slowly looks up; eyes dazed with heroin.

The men sit together; injecting. If someone has trouble
finding a vein, the "doctor" helps; the "doctor" feels a vein, he
gently injects.

We meet Mohammed. He has taken drugs for twenty years,
since he was fifteen. The reporter asks about people dying. Four
went down last year, Mohammed says. But he himself has a protected spirit: he can't die.

He complains about the authorities. They don't go for the
big fish; they hassle the addicts instead. They steal their drugs
and sell them on the street.

Mohammed takes us to meet his mother, Roshana; she sits
on an old sofa in a room, another cracked cement floor. He can't
remember her name. "My mum, she is called Regina," he says
softly, sitting next to her. She corrects him. "Roshana," he repeats,
nodding.

They take out a family album. Roshana has lost four children
to drugs. Her son Ibrahim was an addict and died while taking
drugs, "through the nose and injections," she says. "All my children were taken away by drugs." She is suddenly crying. Two arms
shoot into the frame of the camera to touch her, one is the son,
the other the reporter, or the care worker who has fixed the visit.

I am suddenly crying, too; the futile gentleness of those gestures. And yet it's all we have—kindness, grace, dignity.

"Now I am left with him alone." Roshana rubs her hands,
and raises them in a gesture of despair. "And he is a heavy drug
user." The son murmurs; the voice is not transcribed. The
screen blacks out.

· · ·

Four children have died; one remaining son survives, and he, too, is a drug addict. Who were those children before they got hooked on heroin? Were they unhappy, traumatised, distressed; did Roshana fail them in some fundamental way? Did they fail her? Or were they in the wrong place at the wrong time, falling into something so sweet, so delicious; so soft and loving that they didn't even see their mother's pain?

They were inside the bubble; she was outside.

Heroin, they say, is such an intensely pleasurable experience that you cease to see yourself from the outside: the foolish smile, the sleepy eyes, the dirt and disorder. There is innocence in that, but it also represents a voluntary exile from the world.

"Hashish belongs to the class of solitary joys; it is made for wretched idlers," Baudelaire once wrote.

That is even more true for heroin.

*

Addiction is partly a learnt behaviour, I say to the children. You learn to become an addict. Marijuana is how it starts; you learn to do deals; you learn the music, the mood, the sequence of events, the aftermath.

They don't know how old the drug culture is. Allen Ginsberg was born the same year as my father, in 1926. The opening lines of *Howl* still resonate:

> *I saw the best minds of my generation destroyed by madness,*
> *starving hysterical naked,*
> *dragging themselves through the negro streets at dawn*
> *looking for an angry fix, . . .*

They threw up into bloody toilets; they accused the radio of hypnotism. Their madness and their drugs were entangled like a double helix; a code for an urban culture of rebellion and creativity and destruction.

I think of Rimbaud and Verlaine. *A Season in Hell. Illuminations.* Absinthe and hashish, bitter drunken fights, Verlaine shooting Rimbaud in the wrist. I think of Edie Sedgwick and Andy Warhol, and all the hangers-on taking drugs and having sex and being filmed.

Whole cultures can become addicted, like Russia's dying villages where drinking became endemic, taking years off the national life expectancy statistics, or the current opiate epidemic in the United States, reaching across the class divide.

Social conservatives are terrified. They exercise control because they think transgression is dangerous. I am not one of them. But, you know: they are right. Transgression is dangerous.

The sociologist Erving Goffman has written about how institutions generate their own cultures. But even outside institutions microcultures spring up everywhere—each family, each set of friends, has its own microculture. These cultures may be harmful or beneficial or both. We normalise sets of practices and create habits and traditions. And some of those practices—like taking drugs—can become so normalised that people lose sight of the dangers.

Family members anxiously police the habits of the addict, as far as they can. What happens to them, during the course of the illness? Who do you become if every step out of line—your own and those of others—is recorded and thought about; if every glass of wine brings a hint of anguish; if every sleeping pill brings regret; and the only relief you can find is in long, long walks, and the only excitement you allow yourself is skirting too close to the steep places? Who do you become, policing teenagers; the mess; the beer bottles; the different beds, slept in?

Who do you become when the logical conclusion of every transgression is the drug den and the dead body? Who do you become if you lose faith in the idea of recovery and return?

I am reading Chris Kraus's 1997 autobiographical novel *I Love Dick* with fascination. Do you have any drugs, Dick asks, when Chris comes to seduce him, finally, after pages and pages of unsent letters; after the construction of an academic stalking project which left Dick angry, but intrigued, too. She did have drugs on her, as it happens, quite a choice: a vial of liquid opium, two tabs of acid, thirty Percocet, and some pot.

Those drugs. It occurs to me that I have minimised experimentation in my own life because I so fear where those roads can take you. I have become stricter and stricter, observing Eric having another glass of wine; observing all the steps the kids, now teenagers or older, take away from the straight and narrow, the tidy rooms, the wholesome interests.

Perhaps I've forgotten the dark side of that straight and narrow; the dull repression, the familial police state. I tidy rooms, I set everything straight, as my mother did before me. She started tidying and turning out lights before we'd even left the room when we were teenagers. I don't quite do that. But I do make a fuss about bottles and wrappers and sticky remote controls, even though the bottles are water bottles and the wrappers are for chocolate.

I wouldn't call myself repressed, though. I wouldn't call my mother repressed, either. She was too witty and too ironic for that; her mouth was not set in a thin and disapproving line.

. . .

Sometimes I feel my own mouth set in a thin and disapproving line.

I am haunted by my fear that those small signs—the bottles and wrappers and sticky remotes—are a one-way street to addiction. Perhaps I am so haunted because I missed so many signs before, when we were young, and I was deep in denial. But the distance between that almost mythical space in my mind, Hans and Eva's bedroom, names and contacts of dealers scrawled on the wall, clothes everywhere, trash and dirt—the distance between that space and the ordinary mess of teenage rooms seems so fine to me.

I like to think of myself as broadly nonjudgemental, but of course that's not true. On the contrary, I am constantly judging—as an editor, my days are spent critically reading and editing texts. As a philanthropist I judge grant applications with my fellow trustees on a monthly basis. I send thoughtful and moralising emails—annoying or helpful, who can tell?—to the children about this subject or that. My whole life—all of our lives—are about relying on our judgement, our taste, our instinctive or thought-out preference for *x* over *y*.

I am shaped by moral ideals, by Jane Austen's characters who do, or do not, feel and act *as they ought;* by Agatha Christie's disapproval of murder and murderers, some greedy, some insane, some both (she didn't think much of the distinction); by C. S. Lewis and Laura Ingalls Wilder; by Astrid Lindgren and Tove Jansson. I refill water bottles and store them in the fridge; I rebuild fires with one firelighter instead of three: my thrift is a form of moral control.

In the darkest nights—my sleepless nights—of Hans and Eva's relapse I rotated between Jane Austen, Agatha Christie and C. S. Lewis, and sometimes Rex Stout and Wodehouse, too. Those books are my familiar homes, each their own comforting world, passing through the generations from my grandfather to my father to my sister and me.

At times, too anxious to sleep, I rotated between sleeping pills and Valium, too.

*

Eric always regarded Eva as slightly dangerous and out of control. He thought her and Hans's neglect of the children was immoral, and that their drug taking was irresponsible and selfish. He doesn't really believe that addiction is an illness, and often points out how utterly different Hans and I are. Almost not of the same family. Not obviously siblings. He thinks, also, that I suffer from excessive guilt—guilt about money, guilt about privilege, guilt about Hans, guilt about the children—and encourages me to move on.

How do you *move on*, I sometimes ask.

It takes time, he says.

But time does almost nothing on its own. You need to think it all out.

I have concluded that Hans was imprisoned by his addiction, and that I was imprisoned by it, too. My kidnap fantasy about Hans had become true, but the person in captivity was me. I was in that prison with my allotted food and drink and sleep and walks, observing myself and my family, writing my notes.

. . .

I suspect that drug addicts don't think of themselves as hugely different from other people—it's the only way I can make sense of this. We see them as so vulnerable, so weak; they have crossed over into another world. They see, perhaps, a bit of mess and disorder that will probably stop at some point. Drugs are *fun*, someone said to me once. Of course you don't want to give them up.

How much anguish was there in this whole thing, for Hans and Eva? I genuinely don't know. In the twelve years of their relapse I kept coming back to an imagined drawing of two stick figures—Hans and Eva—inside a bubble. There was colour inside the drug bubble; music and sunshine and flowers. Outside the bubble—"real life"—was a black storm. We were caught up in that storm, in a bleak world of no colour. The children, catastrophically, lost their parents and their home. We all lost our peace of mind. Those thousands of emails, addiction experts, evaluations, reports, conference calls, lawyers, social workers, therapists, and psychiatrists. Those court hearings.

I don't suppose life inside the bubble was really sunny. Drugs create a state of intense contentment, euphoria, excitement, but the bubble is fragile, it drifts in the wind, children pointing, parents smiling, music playing ... then it silently pops and you come back to a dirty room, sick and frightened and despairing.

14

Freud's famous essay about supernatural fears, "The Uncanny," was published in 1919. The first part of the text includes page after page of definitions of the term *unheimlich*, as though the uncanny itself has possessed the text. He then reminds us of the philosopher Friedrich Schelling's definition of the uncanny: "Uncanny is what one calls everything that was meant to remain secret and hidden and has come into the open."

"Uncanny" is a good translation of what *unheimlich* came to stand for, but it misses the twin elements of safe familiarity and dangerous secrets which cling to the root of the German word, which is *Heim*, or "home." The word "homely," with its twin meanings of "cosy" and "ugly," is in some ways the Anglo-Saxon version of the *heimlich/unheimlich* riddle, but of course it doesn't carry the same sinister undertones.

Freud draws attention to other references to *unheimlich*, too. According to the German dictionary of Jacob and Wilhelm Grimm (masters of the uncanny), *heimlich* meant "free from fear," a description of a place that is "free of ghostly influences," "familiar; friendly, confiding."

"Starting from the homely and the domestic, there is a further development towards the notion of something removed from the eyes of strangers, hidden, secret," Freud writes. Thus the *heimlich* and the *unheimlich* intertwine so that *heimlich* came to mean something secret, locked away, inscrutable, or even dangerous. Freud explains this slurring between *heimlich* and *unheimlich* with the idea that the thought or fact which has been repressed is by definition familiar, of the home: the quality of the *heimlich* shimmers around the *unheimlich*. The uncanny is eerily familiar; it is a known entity, repressed and transformed into an unknown one.

The Swedish adjective (and adverb) *hemlig* (secret) and the noun *hemlighet* (a secret) share the linguistic roots of *heimlich*: the Swedish *hem*, the German *Heim*, and the English *home* are the same word. My old German-Swedish dictionary translates *unheimlich* as *hemsk*, "horrible," a word itself derived from *hem*. The other given translations for *unheimlich* are *kuslig* and *spöklig*, "uncanny" and "ghostly." Freud made sense of that strange connection between the home and the secret; the home and the horrible.

*

I think of the premonitions in this book: my mother finding my brother at the village bank that winter morning in the late 1980s; her breakdown and hospitalisation in May 2012; and my own uncanny premonition at that rural airport in Sweden, that ominous sense that something was about to happen.

My mother was repressing her anxiety about an unaccustomed silence, a cessation of communication, and perhaps we all were. Angry and paranoid texts and emails had become the norm; silence was unfamiliar. Our unconscious minds were signalling danger, and for whatever reason our conscious minds mulishly repressed the danger signal.

I write "mulishly" without quite knowing why, but then I remember Tove Jansson's books about the Moomins. She invented a character she named Hemulen. The Hemul was a middle-aged male stamp collector (sometimes botanist), fussy and repressed, who charmingly wore a dress, inherited from his aunt. All Hemuls, male and female, wore dresses, and they all liked order, rules, and fences. Jansson, who belonged to Finland's Swedish minority, would, I'm sure, have been familiar with the German words *heimlich* and *unheimlich;* and I imagine Freud's theories of repression must have been discussed in her bohemian and intellectual Helsinki childhood.

There are unsettling moments in all of Tove Jansson's books, big and small, around which she builds protective walls of kindness, humour, and understanding. The Hemul stands for a quality of repression, but Jansson has tamed him and turned him inside out; he is a fussy collector, a man in a dress. I associate his name with the home—the *hem*—and with the mule, or *mula,* in Swedish. He seems to me to inhabit the mule's stubbornness, as well as some of the Germanic qualities of the *Heim:* order, fences, discipline, repression. The whimsical dress is a flag of inversion, a hint of the reason for repression. Jansson, a lesbian, may have amused herself with that conceit.

But why am I thinking of Tove Jansson and the Moomins, the lyrical and melancholy landscape of coastal Finland, and the sensitive beings that inhabit it? Their feelings are hurt, over and over; the insensitive ones trample all over them. The most terrible and frightening character is the lonely Groke, or *Mårran,* who has no feelings at all, and brings ice and darkness wherever she goes. Moominpappa longs for the sea and grand adventures;

he tinkers with his memoirs; Moominmamma, who embodies some of the detached and semi-mythical maternal quality of Mrs. Moore in *A Passage to India*, makes pancakes for all the little creatures, but is, as I remember her, also somehow existentially alone, without the comforting life lies of the other beings. She sees more clearly than they do.

The Moomin home is a little tower, round like a hobbit dwelling: the Moomins, like hobbits, prize comfort and cosiness over elegance.

It itches at my mind, this idea of a home which does not conceal terrible secrets.

Hans hid Eva's body, and repressed the fact of her death. Funerals are universal; the beliefs and practices are many and varied, but all humans, and probably some prehumans, have disposed of their dead through the ages. When we don't take leave with proper rituals, the dead can come back to haunt or harm us, or they may not find their way to the afterworld. The dead are laid to rest in graves or in monuments; they are launched on boats or buried at sea; they are incinerated or burnt in ritual fire; they are placed on hillsides for the vultures to pick clean or preserved for posterity. When we fail to perform those communal rituals, whatever they are, we break the laws of culture as well as the law of the land. We remove ourselves from the community; we are in self-imposed exile.

We are no longer superstitious, Freud wrote in "The Uncanny," and yet we are not quite securely secular, either: the old beliefs live on in us; we wait and watch for evidence. When Eva cursed me, I half believed that she could genuinely harm me. And part of her may have believed it, too. She wasn't a violent person, but the drugs propelled her into another reality. Freud saw the delusion of omnipotence in black magic as a primitive phase into which modern people can relapse under duress. The old world is still in us; the narcissism of magic contains the delusion of omnipotence.

Eva said she made a wax doll of me. The doll fell and broke its neck. I must be careful. "My witchcraft is going well," she wrote. "See how your neck feels today."

And instead of being careful I galloped up a hill—my own stab at the wild—and my horse fell. I woke up on the ground, severely concussed.

In the dreamy state that followed, meaning, time, and memories warped; I was thrown into acute depression, then euphoria—the garden was dusted with gold; I rested in a warm breeze, dandelion seeds floating. It was intensely peaceful.

The children had been with us for two years. I hadn't seen Hans for a year, and Eva for many months. It was a time of acute anxiety—so much so that the concussion felt like a reprieve. The days were so sunny; they went on forever.

It lasted a week or two. Then real life slowly seeped in through the thinning walls.

*

I tried to teach myself to pray in those years. Having been brought up an atheist I didn't know how—can you think the words, or do you have to say them out loud? Do the words have to form into thoughts in your mind, or can you just be still, nebulous intentions gathering?

Most of my acquired Judaism had melted away, except that I always prayed outside, on my long walks, up to the crest of the fields, then back again. "Green Sussex fading into blue," Tennyson wrote. I looked at the green fields fading into blue; I looked at the trees and the sky and the clouds, and the Jewish tradition which sees God in nature—in a breath of wind over the grass, in a beam of sunlight or a sudden stillness—comforted me. But no words formed, just inchoate supplications.

> *Please*
> *let this be over*
> *let it end well.*

15

Towards the end of the summer of 2012—August 29, to be exact—an article appeared in *The Guardian*.

> Eva Rausing, who was found dead in July at the London home she shared with her husband, an heir to the Tetra Pak fortune, had passed on information about the unsolved 1986 murder of Swedish prime minister Olof Palme, Swedish prosecutors have revealed.
>
> Scotland Yard confirmed on Tuesday night that it had given information to authorities in Sweden, where investigators are now reported as wanting to question Hans Kristian Rausing as a possible witness about the information his wife claimed to have obtained.

The story about Eva and Olof Palme had broken in *Dagens Nyheter*, the Swedish daily newspaper, the day before. Eva, it turned out, had been corresponding with Swedish writer Gunnar Wall, the author of several speculative books about the Palme murder. He contacted the police and the newspaper after Eva died.

·   ·   ·

Prime Minister Olof Palme was shot in the back and killed in Stockholm on the evening of February 28, 1986. He was walking home from the cinema with his wife, Lisbet—they had dismissed their bodyguards. The police still don't know who killed him, or why. It may have been unpremeditated manslaughter. It may have been a case of mistaken identity. It may have been a Swedish far-right conspiracy, or a political assassination by foreign agents.

The police originally believed, apparently on flimsy grounds, that Palme had been assassinated by Kurdish terrorists, but there were many other potential political culprits, including, perhaps most credibly, South Africa. Olof Palme was one of the most vocal international critics of apartheid and donated hundreds of millions of dollars to the ANC—the African National Congress liberation movement—via secret channels, at least one of which had been infiltrated by the infamous South African agent Craig Williamson.

Lisbet Palme, however, eventually identified the gunman as Christer Pettersson, a drug addict with a previous conviction of manslaughter. He seemed to have had no particular motive—one theory was that Palme resembled Pettersson's drug dealer, to whom he owed money. There is a certain cultural logic in the notion that the political leader who had worked so hard to advance equality in Sweden may have been randomly shot on the street, mistaken for someone else. But however improbable it sounds, Pettersson could have had a gun in his possession—the weapon was never found—and he could have pressed the trigger. Lisbet Palme was certain that she recognised him, even though some years had passed by the time he was arrested.

Pettersson was found guilty, but the appeal court later ruled that Lisbet Palme's identification of him was not credible due to police errors—Pettersson had been lined up with a row of plainclothes policemen who were still wearing their regulation black shoes, and Mrs. Palme noticed, and commented on it. Pettersson was released. He was rumoured to have privately confessed to the murder, but later was said to have retracted his confession. He died after a fall in 2004.

Olof Palme died more than thirty years ago. The police bungled the case since the beginning and have not done much better since. In Britain, there would long since have been a public enquiry about the investigation. In Sweden, by contrast, a tailor-made act of Parliament in 2010 abolished the statute of limitations for the most serious crimes. Since the police don't comment on ongoing investigations, there is a lack of information about the Palme case, leading to speculation and conspiracy theories.

*

We are in Sussex; the children are playing outside on the lawn. They are laughing, hitting tennis balls high in the air. A ball veers towards the window, and they see me, mock guilt on their faces, mock stricture on mine. "I'm here!" I shout. They laugh. I'm reading old emails, remembering, remembering.

The first email Eva sent to me on the subject of Olof Palme arrived at 2:15 a.m. on December 31, 2010. It was New Year's Eve, exactly ten years into the relapse. The subject line read "very imporrtant [sic] from Eva and Hans K." The email was long and very angry. She claimed that Hans "had reason to believe" that my father was behind the murder of the prime minister of Sweden. I could stop her going to the police by sending her a coded sign, some flowers, and then we could meet to discuss the return of the children. It was up to me, she said. I had to decide whether I wanted to "protect" my father or not.

I did not respond.

She wrote again on January 18, claiming to know that $30 million had been spent to "take" the children and expressing concern that I had been captured by an imposter. She talked about sending me signs from God, and about her despair. And then, as if in a strange mimicry of the tone in the letters she received from us and from friends, she claimed to miss me, sending *very much love to you always*, adding *I can't wait to have you back*. She signed the email "Eva XXX."

Below those happy and careless *X*s, however, she asked me not to let anyone murder her. She was afraid, she wrote, that my father would attempt to "silence" her. G-d would send me a sign, she said, to encourage me to help her to restore her life and her children.

She wrote again a week later, a heartbreaking and incoherent message. G-d was going to save her, or there was no G-d. She was going to die. But *all will be well*, she repeated over and over.

Eva urgently needed treatment, but she refused all help. The one remaining avenue was to try to have her committed to a mental hospital, but since we were not her nearest relatives we had no power to do so, and our lawyer told us that we would have very little hope of success if we tried.

I think about my old father surreptitiously feeding his dog tidbits under the dining table, reading and rereading *The Hobbit* in Russian to keep up the language. Eva assumed that he was the force behind the court case to gain custody of the children, but he was thinking of other things.

Perhaps it was precisely that slightly indifferent kindness that fuelled her rage.

Eva's first email to Gunnar Wall was sent months later, on June 5, 2011. The subject line read "I know who murdered prime minister Olof Palme." The Swedish newspapers published it after she died, concealing my father's name with an *x*. In the email, Eva claimed that my father was behind the murder of Olof Palme. My brother was supposed to have "discovered" this by chance, and to have been badly affected by it. She wrote that my father thought that Palme threatened his company, which he didn't want to lose. She wrote that she would say more if Wall wrote back.

Eva might not have known or remembered that by 1986—the year of Palme's murder—the headquarters of Tetra Pak had already left Sweden. The reason for the move was the radical political plan to change the ownership of Swedish industry via union-controlled foundations. These trusts would hold shares that industries of a certain size would be compelled to issue on an annual basis, financed by up to 20 percent of revenue, until the union foundations would own 52 percent of the companies, giving them ownership control.

The plan was launched in 1975 by the economist Rudolf Meidner and others, at the request of the unions. Meidner wrote this for the union journal *Fackföreningsrörelsen:*

We want to rob the power from the owners of capital, which they wield precisely in their capacity as owners.

All experience shows that influence and control are not enough. Ownership plays a decisive role. I wish to refer to Marx and to Wigforss: we cannot profoundly change society without changing the structure of ownership. [my translation]

Nordic noir, the crime genre where the villains are always outsiders, often capitalists, is a cultural residue of this political radicalisation. They are the outliers, rejected by the social norms of togetherness.

The Social Democrats lost the 1976 and the 1979 elections to a centre-right coalition. The party continued working on Meidner's plan, however: a joint union and Social Democrat working group issued a report in 1978, and the debate carried on. It looked as if the Social Democrats would implement the Meidner foundations if they won the 1982 election, even though Olof Palme himself was apparently sceptical.

The party did win the election, and the foundations were eventually introduced, albeit in a modified—and ultimately temporary—form. Many families, however, had pre-empted the takeover, and left Sweden before then, bringing their companies with them. My parents left in 1982. Eva's idea, therefore, that Olof Palme had constituted a threat against the company may have been true in the 1970s, but by 1986 it certainly wasn't true anymore. And every newspaper editor in Sweden knew that.

*

I read what I can of the emails from Eva to Gunnar Wall that have been published in various Swedish newspapers. Some were held back, and the rest were redacted. His own part of the conversation has not been published, and he refused my request to see the whole correspondence. In her emails, Eva repeatedly claims that she knows the location of the murder weapon, but never reveals where it was. She contradicts the information that the murder weapon was a calibre .357 Magnum and claims instead that it was .22-calibre revolver. She wrongly insists that Palme had been shot in the neck, and not, as was the case, between the shoulder blades.

Eva told Gunnar Wall about her drug problems, too. She later realised, he said, "that this was not helping her cause." She also regretted, according to Wall, revealing that she had seen the "truth" about the Palme murder in a vision. "Palme is not the first vision but the others have been proven to be 100% accurate," she wrote on June 20, 2011.

Dagens Nyheter asked Gunnar Wall about the discrepancies in Eva's story. "It was obvious to me that Eva Rausing speculated on flimsy grounds about the type of weapon used and how the murder happened," he responded. "But I have met many clever people who have guessed rather widely in exactly that way—most people have no detailed knowledge about the murder. And they can still have important things to say about what they actually do happen to know."

Eva's accusation of murder made all the papers. Sweden was gripped by Nordic noir, and this story had all the ingredients of a crime thriller: an international industrialist, drugs, a woman found dead, and, at the centre, the unsolved murder of the ideological anti-capitalist, the prime minister of Sweden, Olof Palme. And whatever newspaper editors privately thought about my father, whose affairs were in good order, who had no motive, and against whom there was no evidence, the allegation sold papers.

Once the media wheels were turning, Swedish deputy prosecutor general Kerstin Skarp, who was in charge of the investigation, was asked to comment. "We have had information from the British authorities, and she [Eva] has contacted the [Palme police] group before, but otherwise I don't want to say anything about how we work," she said.

Is the information valuable, she was asked.

"We are not making that judgement public," she responded.

Varg Gyllander, press secretary to the police, told the Swedish tabloid *Aftonbladet:*

> "We are aware of this information and there has been a meeting between the Palme group and the prosecutor. But the conclusions of the meeting are secret."

For several years the police Palme group has consisted of just a few people. They sift through and catalogue the leads coming in. They may do more, of course—it's hard to know. There is always a steady trickle of Palme speculation in the Swedish press, and the police response is always the same: they do not comment on ongoing investigations. There is little or no transparency, and the serious tone of the no-comment policy has the curious effect of lending credibility to any claim, however outlandish it may be.

Conspiracy theories thrive where there is no clear information, and the police policy of no comment, perhaps inadvertently, has a creeping fictionalising effect.

In London, *The Times* published Eva's allegation on the front page and a two-page spread inside the paper. I called the then editor when I saw it and asked him whether, when he saw the emails from Eva, he really thought of her as a credible witness. Well, he said. It was obvious that she was somewhat—I can't remember the term he used. "Disturbed," perhaps. Let's say disturbed. But, he continued, I thought it was possible that she was disturbed *and* had gotten hold of something important.

That was the gist of it, anyway.

Too many women in history have been accused of being deranged when they tried to tell the truth, or at least their version of the truth. But there's no doubt in my mind that Eva should have been in hospital care at the time when she was writing her incoherent and paranoid emails.

"They killed the prime minister of Sweden and they will not hesitate to get rid of me," Eva wrote to our lawyer in late spring 2011. "STOP the spread of this evil. They will rule over the lives of others more and more with thier [*sic*] money and will kill those who stand in their way. It becomes easy for them."

She added that everything she wrote or said was being monitored; that she was drugged by her security staff, and that she was sending supernatural signs to make our lawyer believe her.

She was not well. But since she was an addict, inhabiting that dangerous territory between mental illness and free will, between compulsion and volition, she could not be forced into care. She couldn't be coaxed into hospital, and she was not likely to be sent to prison for drug possession. Because she was from a well-known family, the emails to Gunnar Wall became a news commodity. He had the emails for more than a year before he released them: they only became valuable after she died.

·   ·   ·

In September 2012 the British tabloid *The Mail on Sunday* published another story about Eva: EMOTIONAL LETTERS REVEAL BIZARRE FRIENDSHIP BETWEEN TRAGIC HEIRESS EVA RAUSING AND JAILED KILLER . . . AND HOW SHE TOLD HIM "I FEAR FOR MY LIFE."

The prisoner in question was convicted of conspiracy involving drugs and murder. From prison, he wrote to several high-profile drug addicts, including Eva. Her letters, the article stated, made "the remarkable allegations that a well-known businessman had paid for the assassination of Swedish prime minister Olof Palme in 1986, and that she feared somebody would murder her." The authorities in Sweden were said to be "taking seriously Eva's allegations regarding the killing of Olof Palme, and now want to question an unidentified man in Britain who she claimed was the source of her information."

I read what they publish of Eva's letters to the prisoner. Her knowledge about the Palme murder came to her in a "mind wave," she wrote: "One morning, I woke up and looked over at my husband, who was still asleep, and I swear, the thought came to me loud and clear."

"I'm scared!" she added. "What I think that they could do is come into the house, gas me with some sort of sleeping gas, then they could deliberately give me an overdose of some drug or other and then, worst of all, they leave a note in what looks like my handwriting. Help! I know this sounds very far-fetched and completely paranoid but I swear to you these people are capable of anything."

"This is not happening," I said to Eric.

"It's happening," he responded. "It's happening."

.   .   .

A few days later, on September 5, 2012, *Dagens Nyheter* reported that Gunnar Wall had finally established contact with my brother. Hans had sent Wall a text dismissing Eva's Palme story as "completely untrue." It was, he wrote, a "conspiracy theory" with "no basis in reality."

Despite my brother's text, the newspaper speculation refused to die, and it wasn't clear what the police were doing, if anything. I worried about the police silence, and how, in the absence of information, media speculation carried on. In the autumn of 2012, therefore, I contacted the Swedish police to tell them some of the context of Eva's emails to Gunnar Wall and about her drug addiction. I thought that if the police understood the background to the accusation, they could at least make a decision one way or another about how to handle it.

The policeman listened as I talked. He was a good listener. He said that he had unsuccessfully tried to reach my brother to interview him, and then he tried to persuade me to make a formal statement instead. I initially resisted, but over the following months he argued that the tabloids wouldn't stop until the police had a formal statement from a Rausing family member, which would then enable them to close this line of investigation. He presented it as a formality.

I finally agreed. On July 25, 2013, over a year after Eva's body had been found, I emailed him to say that I would be in Stockholm the following month and could meet him then. We set a date and a time. Five days later, on July 30, the tabloid *Expressen* published the following front-page headline:

SIGRID RAUSING TO BE QUESTIONED ABOUT THE PALME MURDER

A friend in Sweden sent me a link.

Kerstin Skarp, deputy prosecutor general, issued her usual comment: "We don't comment on what we do or don't do. We don't comment on individual cases."

The Swedish tabloid *Aftonbladet* republished the story on the same day. Throwing legal caution to the wind, they were the first tabloid to name my father:

> A year before her death Eva Rausing identified her father-in-law, Hans Rausing, as being responsible for the murder of Olof Palme. Now her sister-in-law Sigrid Rausing will be questioned by the Palme group.

I emailed my contact in the police the same day: "That was quick, the leak. I suppose it came from your office. Considering that I have nothing to add to what I have already said it might be better if we don't meet."

On August 21, almost a month later, he finally wrote back. He was genuinely sorry about the leak, he said. He had no explanation for it. He reminded me, also, that Swedish whistle-blowing legislation meant that the police are not allowed to find out how the media gets its information. He was hoping we could talk more.

I did not reply.

The tabloids took a fact—I had volunteered to talk to the police—and twisted it: I was to be "questioned," or "interrogated" (the word is the same in Swedish) by the police. It was as though I had become an accomplice, caught up in this surreal crime fiction. All the tabloids, and many publications I had never heard of, picked up the story.

· · ·

SIGRID RAUSING TO BE QUESTIONED ABOUT THE PALME MURDER
Like the article on Facebook.

The pages have been shared and tweeted many times.

*

I think about my dream of walking into a Copenhagen café, the relief of anonymity and then seeing my name, on the menu blackboard: RAUSING PAID TOO MUCH. I woke up from that dream thinking about this book, about our family seclusion and fear of publicity; our conviction that the world was and is a hostile place. Many articles have been published over the years in Sweden about the Rausing family's privacy, some of them making judgements about my grandfather in particular, including uninformed speculations about my uncle Sven's condition having been caused by patriarchal oppression, or about how he was "hidden" from view. The idea that we are secretive, that we "hide"—ourselves and one another—is so entrenched.

This story has many parts, but much of it has to do with what is hidden and what is revealed; with privacy and with publicity. We were brought up to fear exposure and to shun publicity but the more we hid the more we seemed to have something to hide, our wish for privacy construed as secrecy.

I once inadvertently blurted out the Palme story at a *Granta* magazine editorial meeting. We were discussing a proposed piece on the murder. I knew, even as I spoke, that this was not a good idea, but once I began I couldn't stop.

"I hope I don't have to tell you that of course my father is innocent," I finished lamely, to a slightly stunned silence, which ended only when one member of the group, not an editor, unexpectedly took charge by emphatically saying, "No, of course not," and smiling sunnily.

He refused to inflict pain: an unexpected relief. It reminded me of the Milgram experiments. But why was I thinking about Milgram? His famous experiment, set up in the wake of the Eichmann trial in Jerusalem (1961), was designed to test how far ordinary people were willing to go, to inflict pain on others in obedience to authority. The "teachers"—the subjects of the experiment—were meant to teach word pairs to the "learners." The "teachers" were informed that the experiment was about whether punishment was an effective learning aid. If the answer was wrong, they had to punish the "learners" by inflicting electric shocks of increasing voltage.

The experimenter had a sequence of four prompts for the "teachers," who naturally tended to hesitate when they heard the "learners" screaming and begging them to stop after the shocks:

> *Please continue.*
> *The experiment requires that you continue.*
> *It is absolutely essential that you continue.*
> *You have no other choice, you must go on.*

Twenty-six out of forty "teachers" in the first experiment cooperated with the experimenter by inflicting a series of shocks which they believed to be painful or even dangerous to the "learners." It is slightly unclear how many of the subjects in fact saw through the experiment and carried on anyway—some of them subsequently claimed that they thought it was simply funny. That may be true. But of course there is a significant cultural incentive in distancing yourself from association with Nazi officials, those cogs in the machinery whose confession to the crime (or virtue) of obedience, not moral responsibility, sickened the world. Whatever the case might be, the conclusion— that people are likely to obey authority figures, even if it means inflicting pain—was widely accepted.

But why was I thinking about it, then, in that *Granta* meeting? Perhaps because I felt that we, too, were unwittingly participating in a version of the Milgram experiment. There was an audience beyond us, a circle of journalists and editors and readers observing our family drama. Like Milgram's subjects we were shamed, and judged.

In the private psychodrama of the courtroom, too, we had been accused of inflicting pain, of oppressing innocent victims, of taking action against two parents so clearly disabled by drugs, so obviously the underdogs in this sorry tale. We were the alpha dogs, the guilty ones.

And like the "teachers," we dutifully carried on.

Please continue.
The experiment requires that you continue.
It is absolutely essential that you continue.
You have no other choice, you must go on.

"Guilt" in Swedish is *skuld*, which has a dual meaning: "guilt" and "debt." The English word derives from the Middle English *gilt* and the Old English *gylt*. It is related to "gold," to the German *Geld* (money) and the Gothic *gild* (tax): the word "guilt" throws a shadow of money, of debt, of owing. If you were guilty, you had to pay for what you had done. It seems right, etymologically, that the wealthy, the gilded ones, should be guilty.

I am reading Jean Rhys, *Good Morning, Midnight*. One of the characters in that melancholy book, set in postbohemian 1930s Paris, is a Russian in exile, or perhaps he's from Ukraine. "As things are now," he says, "I wouldn't wish to be rich or strong or powerful. I wouldn't wish to be one of the guilty ones. I know I am not guilty, so I have the right to be just as happy as I can make myself."

The line speaks to me.

I search the website of the Swedish tabloid *Aftonbladet* for "Eva Rausing" and find a neat row of headlines, page after page of stories. You could tell the whole story from the headlines, going backwards in time:

TRAGEDY IN THE SWEDISH UPPER CLASS

HANS KRISTIAN RAUSING'S COSY TIMES WITH NEW WIFE

LIFE HAS TURNED FOR RAUSING

HANS KRISTIAN RAUSING REMARRIES

RAUSING LEAVES THE HOUSE WHERE WIFE DIED

CELEBRITIES' PALME THEORIES

EVA RAUSING WANTED TO BE BURIED IN SWEDEN

RAUSING LOSES BROTHER TO DRUGS

STRONG STORY — DEATH, DRAMA AND ADDICTION

HE STILL KEEPS HIS EVA NEAREST HIS HEART

READY FOR A NEW LIFE — WITH LUXURY GYM

THE LIVES OF SWEDEN'S RICHEST FAMILIES

RAUSING FAMILY BREAKS THE SILENCE

EVA RAUSING'S HUSBAND: I SAW HER DIE

"I KNOW SHE STRUGGLED"

SUSPECTED OF MURDER OF WIFE

ELITE FORCE WERE GOING TO STOP EVA RAUSING FROM
    USING DRUGS

COULD TAKE DRUGS FREELY—GOT HIS MILLIONS ANYWAY

HE LIVED—WITH HIS DEAD WIFE

THE KING WAS HER FRIEND

THEY WERE DRIVEN TO A BITTER FEUD

POLICE HUNTING EVA'S DRUG DEALER

HOW THE RAUSINGS BUILT THEIR BILLIONAIRES'
    IMPERIUM

EVA RAUSING, 49 [SIC], ABOUT HER STRUGGLE WITH
    DRUGS

EVA RAUSING COULD HAVE BEEN DEAD FOR A WEEK

"WE ALL THOUGHT IT WOULD HAPPEN"

THEIR DOWNFALL WAS DRUGS

ROYAL FAMILY MOURNS THEIR FRIEND

EVA RAUSING'S DEATH—A MYSTERY

HERE EVA RAUSING WAS FOUND

SOURCES: "EVA MAY HAVE BEEN DEAD FOR A WEEK"

RAUSING'S FAMILY: WE ARE DEEPLY SHOCKED

CREATED FORTUNE FROM MILK PACKAGING

EVA RAUSING FOUND DEAD

I DEEPLY REGRET IT

16

"I have decided to go to treatment!" Eva wrote in January 2012 to her pen pal in jail, adding:

> Part of me is so pleased and happy to be taking steps at long last to start to free myself from this horrible, horrible prison that I am locked into.

She did go to treatment, but not until April.

She went to a rehab in California. Let's call it Breeze. I look at the website. *Addiction ends here*, it says. There is a photograph of a beautiful mother hugging a daughter, a therapist looking on, smiling. The image changes to a yacht on a blue sea; then a garden with palm trees overlooking the sea; then a woman swimming in a pool; a night scene; a tennis scene; a check-in scene. Every face, every body, is beautiful. No one looks like an addict. It's a fantasy of wealth: this is what money can do.

> *Perched over the Pacific Ocean our five magnificent estates elegantly stretch across ten acres of Malibu coastline, offering you the perfect setting to heal your body, mind, and spirit. For*

over ten years, Breeze has stood out as a shining example of non-12-Step, luxury addiction treatment.

Inside the magnificent grounds at Breeze, you'll find the most comprehensive and sophisticated treatment programs in the world.

I read the website, compulsively. I read it cynically, knowing the limits of what money can do. I read it to see where Eva was that last week.

Why You Should Choose Breeze Drug
and Alcohol Rehab Center.

We know this is an important decision. We encourage you to compare Breeze to any other center in the country. After comparing their fact sheet to ours we are 100% confident you will not find a better facility anywhere in the world.

JCAHO Accredited—only 6% of the nation's rehab centers earn this honor
Forbes magazine's "Most Luxurious Places to Dry Out" List
Rated "Number 1 Rehab in The World" by Healthcare Global
Non-12-Step, holistic approach to addiction recovery
55+ hours of one-on-one treatment per client, per month
16 hours of semi-private treatment per client, per month (3 on 1)
127 Staff members
4-to-1 Staff-to-client ratio (the highest in the country)
24 Hours a day/7 days a week of LVN (licensed vocational nurses) on site
22 different treatment therapy methods

10 therapists assigned to each client
10 acre campus on a bluff overlooking the Pacific Ocean
*5 luxury estates to choose from. All with ocean view accom-
   modations*
2 swimming pools and a jacuzzi
North/South Tennis court
Full gym with personal trainers
No chores or humiliating techniques meant to break you down

They break you down and build you up, in some places, or at
least they used to. Addicts who had never worked in their lives
scrubbed lavatories, sometimes with toothbrushes. Did it work?
I don't know. Studies of best practices are still fairly recent in
the rehab field, and tend not to focus on the different types of
therapy available. The 2009 summary of the UK Drug Treatment Outcome Research Study, for instance, makes only one
treatment recommendation: that encouraging patient motivation should be a key factor. Why? Because the study showed
that patients and practitioners believed it to be important.

So what is treatment, this term we use so casually? Open
a centre and give it a name—*Ocean, Hope, Bliss, Journeys, Voy-
ages, Blessings, Transitions, Abundance, Aspire.* Devise a program,
passionate, uniquely tailored, individualized, exclusive, focused on
*family dynamics, treatment decisions, deeper examination, body and
mind.* Or, if you are the National Health Service, allocate the
few rehab places you have in each local area; write the methadone prescriptions; contact the social workers. Be sure to call
your patients "treatment-seekers," to avoid offence and encourage motivation. But what works and what doesn't work? I don't
know. I'm not sure anyone does. This is an industry driven more
by desperation than by medical evidence.

I click to view the Ocean Therapy program. The video

lasts for a minute. We see a yacht cleaving through the waves, a group of beautiful young people on board. A school of dolphins follows, the sun is setting, accompanied by inspirational music. The video stops several times to buffer up in sudden silent breaks. The breaks are curiously apt, like cracks in the façade.

I click on the main tour. It follows "Ben," good-looking, slightly grizzled. He is shown his ocean-view room. I think of Eva, in the room she didn't leave for a week. I look at the comfortable double bed, the TV, the balcony.

I imagine her lying on that bed, watching that TV.

Ben is having acupuncture. The image seizes up; he looks dead. My throat tenses; I feel tears. This man, however, who is in any case an actor, is not dead—he carries on through some of the fifteen modalities: the alternative treatments; the adventure therapy; the hypnotherapy; the life purpose counselling; the nutrition counselling; the ropes course therapy; the marriage and family therapy; the yoga therapy. There are many closures, one after the other.

Ben's dad comes to see him. We know already that Ben suffers from "low self-esteem," intimidated by his father's success. In this scene he tells his father what the issue is; the father smiles and hugs him. Absurdly, I cry again. I think of my father leaning on my arm, his fine irony, his apartness. He could not have done that hug, that smile. He wouldn't have understood or believed in that simple narrative.

My brother always longed for American suburbia. He longed, I think, to live in a world where those simple narratives could be true, where praise came easily and expectations were moderate. Where he would be valued, not judged.

But perhaps those narratives are never true. Especially in American suburbia.

. . .

In the end "Ben" comes home. He is given a heart stone as he leaves, symbolising the rite of passage from addiction. At home, two children stand by the window waiting for him. They run to greet him, to hug him. A blond and polished woman comes, too; they kiss, expensive luggage on the floor.

But this is not in fact the end. In the final scene, Ben is at the head of a table, in an opulent office. He hands out papers; he speaks. The members of the board look impressed; they smile. An older man whispers to another, they nod in appreciation of who Ben has become.

And for all the bland and sanitized commerciality of the video, I am moved. I am moved because knowing where Eva was the week before she died makes me feel closer to her, perhaps closer to her hopes.

Did she have hopes there, with her Valium? "One Valium, and they threw her out," said her mother. But who knows how many Valiums she had, or other drugs.

*

At least the Malibu rehab, for all its luxury, had a strict policy on drugs. When Eva died I heard a rumour that Hans had been a patient for some time at the Stapleford Centre, an addiction clinic in London that had a controversial history of prescribing narcotic drugs to patients who were known addicts, for maintenance, detox, or even pain control. Its founder, Dr. Brewer, was struck off the medical register in 2006 for professional misconduct after a patient died during a so-called home detox involving a cocktail of various drugs. Two other doctors at the clinic,

Dr. Kindness and Dr. Tovey, were also found guilty of misconduct, but were not struck off—Dr. Kindness retired, and Dr. Tovey was allowed to continue to practice under supervision, conditions which were lifted in 2009. The other Stapleford doctors who were charged were cleared of misconduct.

It turned into a very big case for the GMC, the General Medical Council. *The Guardian* reported on it in November 2006:

> The GMC was highly critical of the program, which put the patient in charge of the drug dose and offered medical support only by telephone. Many of its findings relate to the practice of giving patients long-term prescriptions with the result that they had large quantities of drugs, which they may have been tempted to sell.

I think of Eva's letters to her pen pal in prison, dating from 2009. "I do not use 'drugs' in the sense that I do not need to use illegal drugs," she wrote. "I have well-respected legitimate medical doctors who provide all sorts of 'medications.' Medications, I emphasise, NOT drugs."

I don't think Dr. Brewer or his two colleagues intended to do harm to their patients. It's clear from online forums that addicts who had experienced treatment at the National Health Service as authoritarian and judgemental were protective of the clinic. And no wonder: they were not judged, and if they needed drugs, by all accounts they got them. But it could only have been a matter of time before the clinic was hit by a scandal. It was private, and the treatment was somewhat experimental, or at least unorthodox. There were obvious pitfalls everywhere, including

the probability that at least some of the Stapleford patients com-
bined their prescriptions with other drugs.

Perhaps the doctors trusted their patients too much. Patient
stories are often complex and elusive, but addicts, whose mental
world is shaped by extreme needs, habitually tell lies. I don't
want to be moralistic about this—we would all lie to survive.
Addicts lie because they are, by definition, hostage to cravings
they can't control. They lie about their drug use, and they lie
about their lives. The lies are often obvious and crude, childlike claims to innocence—*everything is fine, it wasn't my fault, I
can't remember what happened, they made me do it.* We all have a
profound aversion to being judged: a guilty judgement can lead
to exile, real or metaphorical.

The Stapleford Centre is still open. They are said to have
improved their practices, and judging by their website they now
seem to favour detox with naltrexone, a substance blocking the
effects of heroin. They still, however, offer methadone maintenance treatment, adding this slightly disturbing offer, in paren-
theses: "(but we can transfer patients to other opiates before
withdrawal and we can usually offer maintenance on buprenor-
phine [Subutex] or morphine although they are must [*sic*] more
expensive then [*sic*] methadone)."

Patients seeking treatment need to document proof of ability to pay and to give a deposit, too. "Unlike most other private
treatment centres, we will always give you a range of treatment
options to suit your needs and finances, if finances are a problem
you can always get *payday loans uk.*"

That's a link. I go there. *Instant cash loans when you need them.
Apply for a loan today!* the web page says. These are loans of up
to two thousand pounds for any purpose, at a stated interest rate

of 180.5 percent (variable). *Late repayment can cause you serious money problems*, the site warns, in small letters.

A few weeks later the sentence on the Stapleford website has changed. It now reads simply, "Unlike most other private treatment centres, we will always give you a range of treatment options to suit your needs and finances."

Hans and Eva lived as recluses in those rooms on the second floor where the housekeepers were not allowed access. Sometimes they left food for them on a tray outside the room. When I asked them what Hans and Eva would eat they looked at each other and shook their heads. One of them said they sometimes ate ice cream at night.

If Hans and Eva were prescribed narcotic drugs by medical doctors—how was that supposed to help them?

17

I am remembering that summer of 2012 again.

I was sitting in our house in Sweden, looking out over the sea. The children had just left. I looked for a book to read and randomly opened an old novel, *Storm Over Jamaica* by Richard Mason. Inside I found a postcard addressed to "the boy Hans-Christian [*sic*] Rausing, Kraftstorg 8, 223 50 Lund." It was a 1960s flip effect postcard of two expressionless koala bears sitting in a tree, blue skies behind. Tilt the card, and the koalas look the other way.

I saw that the card had been made by Axel Eliasson's Konstförlag AB Stockholm. This was Sweden's leading manufacturer of postcards until the mid-twentieth century. By the time of this card Axel Eliasson's Konstförlag's heyday was over, though this innovation—lenticular printing—must have been exciting in its time.

My grandfather was in the printing business, too, before packaging, before his first company, Åkerlund and Rausing, and long before Tetra Pak. He probably knew Axel Eliasson, or knew of him, anyway.

Something about that flip effect turns the card from a message to a gift. And the koalas—the person who sent this card must have known us well. My parents went to Australia and brought back two koalas, a soft furry life-size one, with a black plastic nose and claws, and a small carved wooden one. My brother and I exchanged those koalas back and forth for Christmas for years.

I have the wooden koala still. It sits like a little Buddha on a chest of drawers in this room, looking placidly towards the window and the late-summer butterflies outside. For years it was a reminder of my lost brother; an embodiment of loss. When I was too sad to look at it, I put it away in a drawer. Then I'd bring it out again.

Simrishamn 13th March

Dear "Gurre," how are you now. I hope you are well. Everything is fine here, but gosh how much I miss you. Now I have forty different children to look after, so it's a lot of work, but really fun. I will call you later. Hugs, [something illegible] Britt

"Gurre"—my brother's nickname when he was very young. But who is something-Britt? Gun-Britt is the only name I can think of—she must be a forgotten nanny or au pair. Neat old-fashioned handwriting. My mother probably left the card in *Storm Over Jamaica* in Lund and brought the book to our summerhouse to read. She prepared this house for my brother, placing old books on shelves. *Storm Over Jamaica* (who reads it now?) slipped in, the card inside. A message from now to then, the land of the unknowable. I stand in the future, the card in my hand.

I read between the lines that my brother had been ill, as he often was: how are you *now*? My mother worried, I remember that. Dark anxieties fed her own depression after her parents died. But even in her most anxious fantasies about the future, the land of now would have been unimaginable.

Storm Over Jamaica was made into a film, released in 1958, the year of my parents' wedding. Maybe they saw it.

I find it online. The website has given it a tagline which reads: AN ISLAND PARADISE . . . *where all human emotions are exposed under a tropic sun.*

My parents would have been amused by that.

I check, and the actual film poster has "tropical" not "tropic."

The finger wags and wags; I admonish and correct as I read.

*

On the tenth of March 2012 Eva wrote to me for the last time. She was legally no longer allowed to contact me, but I was glad that she did: there was hope in that email. A faint sense of a future. She wrote that she was moving to America, to live with her sister. She was taking back her maiden name, Kemeny. "From your sister in law," she signed off. "Eva Rausing but not for much longer!"

And for the first time in such a long time, she said something kind:

> I can tell you one thing that I know for sure Sigrid and that is that you were genuinely and truly loved by your brother. I'm sure many other people love you very much as well, but I absolutely know for a fact that your brother loved you very much.

That in itself felt like the beginning of recovery.

.   .   .

Within two months she was dead.

But it was in that spirit, I think, that she went to Malibu.

I like to think that she hoped for a new life. But when it came to it she couldn't do it, and instead stayed in her room the whole time she was at the rehab, before being asked to leave for bringing in drugs.

That one Valium.

If that is what it was.

Where was my brother all this time?

I don't know.

He was like a hibernating bear, deep in his addiction.

*

Each summer is different, and each summer is the same.

My notes merge; I struggle to keep the years separate.

I am alone. The sea is still today; the wind has died. For the first time ever I heard the church bells, miles away.

I walk on the common, through the herd of heifers. If I don't look at them I am invisible; they stare at me, but they don't see me. I walk head down.

Last night it thundered on and off, a low rumbling that came to nothing in the end. The weather didn't break: the heat continues. I walk by the sea, on unmarked paths from childhood. Sometimes I stop to swim. I take off my clothes and make a bundle, I put my watch in a shoe. I stare at the cold dark water, cliffs and stones, seaweed, crabs, and huge orange jellyfish like balls of fire.

Geese fly above. I lower myself onto the natural step, the

rock. I hold handfuls of slippery seaweed and propel myself into the water. At times I am afraid. A tern hovers nearby—she attacked me the other day, but now she ignores me, hunting in the shallows. I swim across the bay, feeling only intermittently safe in the velvety dark water.

Perhaps that is the point. I reify my anxiety; I exhaust myself to feel in my body what I feel in my mind.

It's a hot day. We swim off the jetty. There was a grey rock in the water, a slightly odd grey rock. "Uh-oh," said Eric, before I realised what it was. This was not good: a dead seal, upside down, nearly washed ashore. We rang the council. They *might* come later, they said, stressing the "might."

After lunch I looked at the seal again, through the binoculars. The body had flipped and drifted to the other side of the jetty. People were swimming, oblivious. A curious red rose had blossomed on its stomach. I wondered if the rose was the genitals of the seal, looked again, and saw: red guts spilling out of the swollen body into a tight spiral.

*

On Wednesday, February 5, 2014, I saw Hans for the first time since June 15, 2008.

I look at the dates. The years feel so dense, like thick grey snow, melting, refreezing. I can't penetrate them.

Was this all my life?

I hadn't seen him for nearly six years. We had had some limited communication in all that time, but not much. He had walked away from me, and perhaps the truth is that I was beginning to let go of him, too.

Now I was to see him: Hans had invited me and my mother for lunch. She came up from Sussex; I came from our house in London; we had arranged to meet outside his rented flat. I had thought I would be late, because there was a tube strike that day, and so had Hans.

"Park Lane is solid," he texted, or words to that effect. "I am stuck in traffic, may be late."

"Me too!" I wrote back. That friendly exclamation mark. So happy to finally be in the same boat.

In the end none of us was late. My mother was waiting in her car as I pulled up. Her driver opened the door, and I helped her out. I thought of all the cathartic family meetings at the rehab in 1989. *God grant me the serenity to accept the things I cannot change, the courage to change the things I can, and the wisdom to see the difference*, we had chanted in unison, Sunday after Sunday, a faint sense of bitter bewilderment in the room.

Here we were, twenty-five years later. My mother had mobilised all her strength, her solid generational determination in the face of this monumental meeting, after years of absence. By now he was not only her son and my brother. He had also become a symbol: the dense centre of all the years of sleepless nights, of chaos, of anguish and of grief. Like the medieval concept of the king's two bodies—the body politic, the enduring and abstract power of the king, and the body natural, the king's physical body, subject to human laws of decay—Hans had become dual in my imagination. He was a knowable person, and he was the embodiment of history, of fifteen years of dysfunction.

We rang the doorbell and were admitted by a young man, a minder, I supposed, versatile and discreet. I was glad of his presence, though he disappeared as soon as coats had been disposed of; my mother's walking stick lost and found.

I saw Hans.

I hugged him lightly. I had forgotten his height, his bulk. His hair was greyer, and thinning. He wore a green tweed jacket. He was very pale, with a little stubble. His hands shook.

We walked up a steep staircase; Hans had to help my mother up step by step, pushing and pulling. She had difficulties walking at the best of times; this staircase was almost too much for her. There was loud music on, too, an LP playing. "I found all my old records," Hans said, happily. "They were in perfect condition."

At the end of a long corridor was a photograph of Marilyn Monroe, and maybe an Andy Warhol, too.

Hans turned the music down. We sat and talked for a while.

I wondered about his comment about the records. Did he mean that he had found his way back to his old life, that his life was still there, intact, waiting for him?

Speculation, I know. But there was much to speculate about. I watched for signs. And those signs—Andy Warhol and Marilyn Monroe, loud music—are not neutral in terms of drugs, in terms of celebrity and notoriety, in terms of life and death. It would be difficult to argue that they meant nothing, in this context.

But my own watchfulness is a sign too. I know that. It's his addiction but it's my addiction too.

We talked about this and that. We talked about nothing in particular. The emotional black hole, that dense physical centre, turned out to be a surprisingly bland space, occupied with fish and sorbet, with water, fizzy or still, and with a small paper cup of pills for my brother. Briefly, the symbolic centre transferred to that small waxed-paper cup, folded at the sides, containing, I suppose, enough morphine to put me or my mother to sleep until the following morning. Morphine detoxes are very slow—they have to be, to avoid nerve damage.

We drank coffee, served by the same housekeepers, still there, after all those years.

Hans had to leave by 2:30 p.m.

My mother and I left together. We stood in silence outside her car. There had been too much to say, and we hadn't said any of it. We had reverted to type; politely passing the water, commenting on the fish, sipping the coffee.

"He was nervous," my mother suddenly said. "We must remember that."

*

In the autumn of 2012 I received an email from someone I didn't know. He had something to tell me, he said. It was about Eva. I remembered who he was, and after some hesitation agreed to meet him at his place of work near Piccadilly.

It was 6:00 p.m., and the place was empty, apart from my correspondent, a tired-looking man in his fifties. We talked. Eva was "paranoid," he said, "but I liked her. She was a bright girl. I felt a bit sorry for her. We've all done drugs, haven't we?"

I nodded, silently. He carried on. Eva had to give urine samples, he said. So his wife did it for her. She had to take some other drug that Eva was on and wait for it to metabolise before peeing into a cup.

The drug testing must have been part of those "rehabilitative or reparative conditions," issued by Judge Timothy Workman in 2008. That "very sensible decision," which had come to nothing. Or not nothing: a couple, waiting in a grand house, unknown medicines metabolising in the wrong body. It meant something to them, I presume. Some misplaced loyalty, or kindness, or both, or more.

"She left me this package and to tell you the truth I just want to get rid of it and walk away. I really like your family, and I don't want any trouble, and it's on my mind, bothering me. Here it is."

The envelope was open. I looked at him, at his tired eyes, his salt-and-pepper hair.

"Yeah, I did read it. You know."

The envelope was in my hand. I looked at the contents. I thanked him. Then I climbed down the stairs to the street and walked for some time in the early autumn twilight, until Eric picked me up.

I showed him the papers in the car.

It was a photocopy of the names and contact details of all Swedish ministers of 2009. There was an empty sheet of Eva's personal letterhead and an empty envelope. And there was a letter printed on white paper, making another false allegation against my father, an allegation that had nothing to do with Olof Palme.

She ended the letter: "I am sorry for the necessity to do this but Hans Rausing has harmed me badly and I believe that he deserves to be caught, if not for what he did to me then for this. I wish you well and am glad to offer my help if you need it."

I don't know if she ever sent it and, if so, when, or to whom.

I still wonder about her rage against my father—that angry grudge against someone who had always been kind to her. She had a skewed perception of his power, and of the power of money; a patriarchal and conservative bent clashing with her teenage rebellion.

I think of Patty Hearst holding a machine gun, then asking for eyeliner in prison. Or so the story goes.

*

The summer of 2014 Eric and I took the ferry over to Denmark to see the Emil Nolde exhibition at Louisiana, the art museum on the coast north of Copenhagen. It was an extraordinary show, disturbing and impressive. Eric, disliking Nolde's political ambiguity, his Nazi leanings, walked outside in the grounds. I came, alone, to the painting *Adam and Eve Banished from Paradise* (1919).

Adam and Eve, stout and graceless, sit naked on the ground, side by side, their eyes that strange intense Nolde blue, no whites. Between them the snake curls up a purple pole. A lion emerges from the background, white teeth showing, a hungry, bitter face.

The expressions of Adam and Eve are so remarkable that you don't quite notice the dissonant colours, the garish clash of red earth and purple tree trunk. There is no doubt that they are lost: nothing I have seen better captures the Fall than that wide-eyed silent stare, that visible shock, that mute stubbornness.

They were no sooner out of their blissful abode than a paralyzing terror befell them, my old Jewish Encyclopedia of 1901 tells me.

Unaccustomed to the earthly life and unfamiliar with the changes of the day and of the weather—in paradise an eternal light had surrounded them—they were terrified when the darkness of night began to fall upon the earth, and the intercession of God's word was necessary to explain to them the new order of things. From this moment the sufferings of life began; for Adam and Eve were afraid to partake of earthly food, and fasted for the first seven days after their expulsion from paradise, as is prescribed in Talmudic law before an im-minent famine. (Volume 1, page 179)

Eve seems slightly more blind in the painting, staring without seeing, hypnotised or exhausted. Adam looks over to the left, with more anxiety, and more consciousness. The snake looks foolish and drunk; the sinister lion is coming closer.

This was the story of Hans and Eva, too, tempted by the snake in paradise, then banished. Tempted not by knowledge—humanity, it seems to me, is redeemed by the fact that Adam and Eve's temptation was a desire for moral knowledge, the capacity to distinguish right from wrong—but instead by something that might make paradise even more heavenly, something that would lead not to consciousness and intelligence but to blissful unconsciousness.

Eve was tempted by the serpent, who told her that if she and Adam ate the forbidden fruit their eyes would be opened, and they *would be as gods, knowing good and evil* (Genesis 3:5).

Hans and Eva partook of another forbidden fruit to re-enter paradise and forget the ethical distinctions they knew.

There is amnesia at the heart of drug addiction.

Floating in the oblivion of heroin and the euphoria of crack and cocaine, Hans and Eva didn't want out, they wanted in. They were in exile, searching for home. The drug den, the bubble, was Eden.

*

Last summer I saw an adder on the dirt road that runs along a part of the common. We sometimes cycle along that road to the village, passing a row of small summerhouses, all as familiar to me as the ceiling of my psychoanalyst's office; the random dots that I line up into gloomy squares as I talk and talk. I was walking home, past the farmhouse with the French flag and the 1960s glass front. I walked on, past the next house, the glass house where the parents of an old boyfriend still spend their summers. I walked, looking down to avoid being seen, when the adder emerged from the stone wall behind some roses. It was about two feet long, slim and agile, with a precise olive-green diamond pattern on its back, a little tongue flicking out of a lined mouth.

Now I wonder if the tongue was really there, but I can see it in my mind's eye, on that warm sandy road, the stone wall, the glass house beyond.

Eric and I took the same walk a few days later, and I told him about the adder. I didn't expect to see it again, but it emerged from the same place, the same olive diamond body against the warm sand. We jumped towards each other like Hansel and Gretel in the forest, laughing slightly hysterically at our own nerves. We were laughing at me, at my pretend nature lore, my bravado; and laughing at him, at the sudden absence of macho courage, his mock-falsetto jump.

The snake slithered off. But it remained in my mind as a threat—and why did it emerge in front of me, twice?

I remembered my mother raking the bushes by our house where an adder had been seen, my father standing by with his gun, ready to shoot. There is a photograph of it: she wore her long 1970s crazy-pattern turquoise dress with plastic beads on wide sleeves, hair short and permed; he was in a short-sleeved shirt and panama hat. They never found that adder.

But death was there, even in this clean wild place (our pointer gently carrying dying rabbits, eyes gummed shut with myxomatosis; the dead seal, rose intestines curling into tight spirals). Repulsion was there (sticking my hand into the hole in the ground to turn the tap of the fountain; hole crawling with earwigs).

The snake was real. That green-and-olive diamond pattern on the sandy road, the stone wall, the house beyond: the snake was not a symbol or a message. It was not *meant*, I must remember. The snake had its own world, its own thoughts and preoccupations, to do, I presume, with food, with smells, with danger, with the pleasant heat of the sandy road.

I want to see the snake before the snake sees me, to catch a glimpse of that other world.

*

In the summer of 2015 a friend took me to see Anne Carson's version of Euripides's *Bakkhai*, playing at the Almeida theatre in Islington. The Bakkhai, or maenads, are the female followers of Dionysus, also known as Bacchus. Crazed and murderous, they follow Dionysus into destruction. King Pentheus is lynched and torn to pieces by his own mother, Agave, who has joined the cult—it is a plot devised by Dionysus to punish Agave with grief, with guilt, and with exile for her initial disbelief and disrespect.

We sat near the stage in the small theatre. Towards the end of the play Pentheus's body parts were assembled and placed on a blue tarpaulin on the stage.

I froze. The blue tarpaulin. The body parts.

Islington's Upper Street near the theatre is lined with bars, people were drinking outside, there was vomit on the pavement. We walked faster and faster until I found a taxi and got in, leaving my friend, who was going in a different direction, on the street.

I felt guilt.

Only later did I make the connection: the play, the street, the drinking, had upset me.

Only later did I forgive myself for leaving so abruptly in that taxi.

*

I think of my lovely dog Leo, the vet injecting his leg. Leo dying in my arms.

I sat with him on the steps outside the kitchen where I used to wave goodbye to the children with his paw. I fed him small pieces of meat; he took them so gingerly, so slowly, deaf now, and almost blind.

The vet injected him; he shuddered, and died.

The wind touched his fur; it moved in the wind so that he seemed alive still, for so long.

We wrapped him in a sheet. I couldn't bear to think of him buried in the cold dark earth, so he lay on the sheet by the grave we had dug, the hole we had dug, for a long time.

I had to know that he was really gone.

We live, and then we die.

Things end.

18

My life is made up of rooms. I walk from room to room, each shift in atmosphere slightly jarring. In each room I tell the story.

The rooms are actual rooms, the rooms are different languages, and the rooms are different relationships.

I see my complicity, my guilt. I see my tiredness, my hopelessness; my false moral superiority, my finger wagging, wagging. I regret everything.

I see my guilt, I see the guilt of others. All of us are guilty, all of us are complicit.

People offer absolutions: I am embarrassed by their attempts to comfort me, their clumsy well-meant offers:

You did your best.

Where would the children have been without you.

They are so lucky to have you.

This is not reasonable of me, I know, but I want people to understand the nature of what the children went through. Of course it would have been worse without us. But they were hardly lucky.

. . .

I try to understand this catastrophic breakdown, this strange inversion of wealth: here's a double-fronted townhouse, with oil paintings and marble, with paint effects and chintz curtains, with solid sofas, old rugs, Victorian desks and Georgian chairs, with strong brass rods holding the stair carpet in place; that thick and pleasant stair carpet.

Those strong brass rods.

And inside all that solid wealth, inside that slightly stiff combination of new and old, is a drug den.

A locked room.

*

Sometime that autumn of 2012, I saw a documentary about experimental processes of rotting in a closed room, visible behind glass. Many substances rotted, and the camera focused on each in turn. Insects appeared seemingly out of nowhere, life out of death. I was tired; it was mildly interesting. And then the focus shifted to the carcass of a pig, left on the side. I suddenly started weeping uncontrollably as the pig's body deteriorated. I switched off the TV, alone in the house except for my sleeping nephew.

I rang Eric. I cried so much I couldn't speak. *How could they*, I tried to say.

How could they show something like that on TV?

I didn't see that my reaction was unusual.

And then, slowly, another era began. Think of dawn on a cloudy day: the dark feels as if it will go on forever, but suddenly you realise there is a lifting, or dispersal, of the dark.

There is my sister, and her husband. There is my husband,

and my parents. We sit and stare at one another. How pale we are, how tense our faces. We sit in a circle, in a cave. There are shadows on the walls of the cave; real life goes on somewhere else.

One by one we crawl out, blinking in the sun. We smell the morning air, we stand up on unsteady legs.

This twelve-year episode of intense anxiety; of court cases; of social workers and lawyers and judges; of self-proclaimed experts and psychiatrists; of abusive letters and fear and shame and constant red alerts already seems not quite real.

*

I tell my father I am writing a book about what happened. It's summer; he is sitting in his rocking chair, reading, watching the sea, looking out for hares.

"Good," he says. He gestures at the common, at the sea. "Then it won't be just fragments, like a dream."

I try to finish the text, but something is missing. I fear I have redacted too much—real life was so much more painful and confusing and stressful than this book. You write and write. You hone, you edit. Each phase takes you to a different place; you process the memories, over and over.

This is a representation of the story, not the actual story.

I think about where it began: "Now that it's all over I find myself thinking about family history and family memories; the stories that hold a family together, and the acts that can split it apart."

"Now that it's all over"—what hopes I had. *Language is indeed a machine that continually amplifies the emotions.*

But still: my brother is remarried, and in recovery. He is rebuilding his relationship with his children, and with all of us.

*

Daniel graduates from school. My brother comes; Lisbet and Peter come. Daniel's father is here, with his new wife. Daniel plays football with his friends; they shoot the ball at the ruined monastery wall; they pose for endless photographs; they smile blankly, shocked that this mythical day has actually arrived.

This is more than we could have hoped for, this reprieve, this happy scene. The swifts are diving in the wind, my brother leans back in his green folding chair holding now an olive, now a piece of mozzarella; he talks to my ex-husband about a clinic in Austria they both know; they laugh. I listen to the echoes of conversations long ago, when I was married to my ex-husband and my brother was married to Eva and the people we are now married to were unknown to us and to each other.

*

About a month before this, Eric and I had seen the *Unfinished* show at the new Met Breuer in New York. I was finishing this book and was interested in the idea of the unfinished. I had imagined that unfinished works might be as interesting as finished ones, perhaps in fact even more poignant—more emotional, revealing, and raw. But most of the paintings on show—by famous artists all—felt oddly lifeless to me. That thing, the touch that denotes that a work of art is done, was lacking; the unfinished petered out.

I almost wished I hadn't seen these paintings. There was Klimt's posthumous portrait of Ria Munk, so similar to his earlier portrait of Adele Bloch-Bauer, the glorious *Woman in Gold* now at the Neue Galerie a few blocks north. Same pose, same construction. *Woman in Gold* is prewar; the portrait of Ria Munk, who had died long before Klimt could finish it, dates from 1917–18. The war was still raging; there were tired maimed soldiers in hospitals and on the streets; people were hungry in Vienna. The painting feels like a sketchy pastiche; like ersatz food; like rationing and disillusion.

There's Sargent's *Two Girls with Parasols*, faces blank blobs, crude hands like birds' beaks. There is a Lucian Freud self-portrait, a pencil drawing only partially filled in with paint, a grotesque mask over the bones—I think of painted faces and concealed death, the process of creation and the process of disintegration.

I conclude that I can't get away with the unfinished. It's not enough: I must tie it all together, finish the stitching.

And yet I also like the tradition of investigations, of analysis, of children tearing their toys apart to understand the mechanism, the pieces on the carpet, the missing clues.

Maybe this book can't be finished partly because I can't decide which tradition I like better; where I belong.

More than that, I am hesitant to release it into the world, to have this sad legacy picked apart once more. Better to forget, perhaps.

But then my book will be unfinished, like the paintings in the show. And people will never know that once, long ago, Eva and I sat side by side, a child playing behind us, throwing her head up to the sky.

"That's me!" my eldest niece exclaims when I show her the photograph, asking her if she can tell who the child is. So then I know: it must have been around the year 1999 or 2000. The cusp of Eva's relapse. It was still invisible; soon we would know.

Afterword

As I was writing this book, drug overdosing became the leading cause of accidental death in the United States. Thousands of people in Britain, too, lose their lives to drugs every year. Not all the people who die are addicts, but probably most of them are, leaving a trail of sadness and devastation behind them: broken promises, broken homes, broken lives. This book is for the people they leave behind.

It is dedicated to Hans and Eva's four children. For legal reasons, they cannot be named in the book. That is one of the many reasons why the text remains as partial and unfinished as it is, since these young people, alongside my own son Daniel, were, and are, an indelible part of my life.

I thank them for their patience, their humour, and their courage.

Acknowledgements

Thank you:

Eric Abraham, Lisbet Rausing, Robin Desser, Simon Prosser, Albert Bonnier, Sarah Chalfant, Andrew Wylie, Stephen Grosz, Johanna Ekström, Rosalind Porter, Domonic Barber, Jennifer Kurdyla, Hermione Thompson, Emma Duncan, Hans Jürgen Balmes, Max Porter, Adam Nicolson and Elizabeth Wedmore.

A NOTE ABOUT THE AUTHOR

Sigrid Rausing is the editor of *Granta* magazine, and the publisher of Granta Books. She is the author of two previous books, the monograph *History, Memory, and Identity in Post-Soviet Estonia*, and *Everything Is Wonderful*, a memoir about living on a collective farm in Estonia, which was short-listed for the Royal Society of Literature Ondaatje Prize. She is a member of the Cultural Council of the University of Lund and an Ambassadors Council member of the Scholars at Risk Network. Rausing has a PhD in Social Anthropology from University College London, and is an honorary fellow of the London School of Economics and St. Antony's College, Oxford. She lives in London with her husband, film and theatre producer Eric Abraham.

A NOTE ON THE TYPE

This book was set in Janson, a typeface long thought to have been made by the Dutchman Anton Janson, who was a practicing typefounder in Leipzig during the years 1668–1687. However, it has been conclusively demonstrated that these types are actually the work of Nicholas Kis (1650–1702), a Hungarian, who most probably learned his trade from the master Dutch typefounder Dirk Voskens. The type is an excellent example of the influential and sturdy Dutch types that prevailed in England up to the time William Caslon (1692–1766) developed his own incomparable designs from them.

Typeset by Scribe,
Philadelphia, Pennsylvania

Printed and bound by LSC Communications,
Harrisonburg, Virginia

Designed by Soonyoung Kwon